"Laraine Harper left a positive mark on t ... es
a very special individual to oversee a cove... ...g willed working girls
and her sense of humor and ability to make the best and the most out of
any situation is reflected in her writing."

— **Wayne Bridge**
CEO, Sin City Chamber of Commerce

"Wow. Talk about Nevada 'off the beaten path'. In *Legal Tender*, Laraine
Russo Harper gives readers a tour of the state's legal brothel industry. Find
out who pays for what — and why — what's on the 'menu' and that it's really true; some men do pay just to talk."

— **Heidi Knapp Rinella**
Author, *Nevada Off the Beaten Path*

"My Red Hat Society chapter visited the brothel out of curiosity and ended
up with an education, as Laraine and one of the ladies answered every question we asked — and even let us get our pictures taken in the S&M room.
Legal Tender is equally enlightening."

— **Olga Scheel**
Member, Red Hat Society

"Legal brothels are legendary establishments in these parts. They would have
to be to lure customers away from the Las Vegas Strip, with all its earthly
delights. And who better to share a brothel's colorful history than the
madam who saw . . . and heard . . . everything."

— **Jack Sheehan**
Author, *Skin City: Uncovering the Las Vegas Sex Industry*

"Totally captivating! I started the book on Friday night and couldn't put it
down until I finished it early Saturday morning. I felt like I had spent the
night with the author telling me her story. I laughed; I cried; I learned. A
real eye-opener!"

— **Carole Buffington**
Businesswoman (with a whole new perception)

"An up close and personal look at what REALLY happens in a legal brothel — and what most brothel owners never want the 'outside world' to know. From the fast money to the moments laughing with each other to the not-so-pretty times too, this is the real story. I have worked in the brothel industry for nine years. The brothel industry has lost a great madam but I gained a true friend in the writer/madam. Funny, who'd have thought I would find such a real friendship in a brothel, but this ol' hooker smiles, even as I write it."

— FAMOUS ALICIA

"Great reading! As a former madam myself, I can honestly say *Legal Tender* is very informative, true to life and totally entertaining. My madam years were the most interesting years I've ever had and enabled me to view life differently. Thank you, Laraine, for educating the 'public sector.'"

— ALOTTA FANZ
Former Madam

"*Legal Tender* is the best way to see the inner workings of what most people don't understand, and call a whorehouse. Reading it, you'll experience the good side of a house, where some great ladies live, work and play — a brothel. I know. I've been there, done that, and got the T-shirt."

— MARK GASSMAN
Customer

"*Legal Tender* is by far the most accurate and entertaining description of the brothel business today. As a brothel owner myself I was happy to see that someone has finally taken the time to enlighten the general public of what really takes place at a brothel. You will be genuinely surprised to learn what it takes to make this controversial industry successful and, at times, laugh out loud as some situations can only take place inside the world of legal prostitution. *Legal Tender* will take you on a journey into the depths of the world of legalized prostitution and what affects it has on people of all walks of life. In the "line-up" of brothel literature, *Legal Tender* tells it like it is with humor and truth."

—BOBBIE DAVIS, OWNER
Shady Lady Ranch

Legal Tender

Legal Tender

True Tales of a Brothel Madam

Laraine Russo Harper

Stephens Press • Las Vegas, Nevada

NOTE FROM THE PUBLISHER: All persons and places portrayed in this book are real. All names in this book are pseudonyms. Nevada and local statutes regulate brothel activities and no endorsement of such activities is intended by this book. The author of this book is solely responsible for the views and content herein.

Editor: Geoff Schumacher
Designer: Sue Campbell
Production Coordinator: Stacey Fott

Cataloging-in-Publication
Harper, Laraine Russo.
Legal tender : true tales of a brothel madam / Laraine Russo Harper.
250 p. ; 23 cm.
The author relates her experiences over six years as a madam at a brothel in Pahrump, Nevada.

ISBN: 1-932173-94-3 (hc)
ISBN-13: 978-1-932173-94-9 (hc)
ISBN: 1-932173-97-8 (pbk.)
ISBN-13: 978-1-932178-97-0 (pbk.)

1. Harper, Laraine Russo. 2. Brothels—Nevada. 3. Prostitution—Nevada. 3. I. Title.

306.74'09793 dc22   2008   2008928762

STEPHENS PRESS, LLC
A Stephens Media Company
Post Office Box 1600
Las Vegas, NV 89125-1600
www.stephenspress.com

Printed in Hong Kong

To my husband, Kevin; my three children, Jennifer, Michael, and Kevin; my doggies, who have always made me look good; my friends in Las Vegas and Bradley Beach; the beautiful ladies of the brothel; and Ed, who I will miss until we meet again.

CONTENTS

Foreword

by

Geoff Schumacher

Nevada has a reputation as a place where "live and let live" is not just a dusty proverb, but a way of life. It started with the adventurous souls who came to the sparse and unforgiving deserts of the Great Basin in the mid-nineteenth century. These pioneers and fortune-seekers tended to be people who chafed at the notion of being told what to do, whether by a government official, law enforcement officer, or religious leader. The central tenet of the frontier lifestyle they embraced was that people can do pretty much whatever they want as long as they don't hurt others.

This philosophy was reinforced in 1931 when the Nevada Legislature passed and Governor Fred Balzar signed a bill to legalize casino gambling. This bold act sparked furious condemnations across the country. In his book *Nevada: A History*, the late Robert Laxalt summarized the national reaction and the Silver State's response:

"The hue and cry was directed at Nevada from all parts of the nation. It came in the form of denunciation from the pulpits, angry speeches in the Congress, and indignation from newspaper editors. If the intent of the moral outrage was to shame Nevada into the paths of righteousness, it failed. All that it accomplished was to make Nevadans defensive, and in the process, bolster an uncertain support within the state's borders for its libertarian laws."

Nevada's radical tolerance extended beyond gambling to include other "sinful" activities, including prize-fighting, quickie divorces, and prostitution. The latter vice did a thriving business in the formative years of the small railroad town of Las Vegas, where "Block 16" was designated as the zone where drinking liquor and paying for sexual favors would be tolerated. Block 16 continued to function as the city's red-light district until World War II, when military leaders at the local air base insisted that the young soldiers not be subjected to such blatant temptations.

While brothels were nudged or shoved out of the newly image-conscious cities, they continued to operate in rural parts of Nevada. There was no state law that explicitly addressed the legality of prostitution — still isn't — but the brothels remained open by the grace of the local sheriff and district attorney.

Of course, this was a tenuous way of doing business. Tired of the nagging uncertainty that moral crusaders could shut him down as a "public nuisance," Joe Conforte, owner of the Mustang Ranch outside Reno, persuaded Storey County politicians in 1971 to create an ordinance legalizing brothels. Other rural counties soon followed Storey's lead, creating ordinances for the licensing, regulation, and taxation of houses of prostitution.

By state law, brothels are not allowed in counties with more than 400,000 population. This affects two of them: Clark (home of Las Vegas) and Washoe (home of Reno). Brothels also are outlawed by local ordinance in Douglas and Lincoln counties and the state capital of Carson City. Eureka and Pershing counties, which do not have any brothels, lack ordinances for or against.

That leaves ten Nevada counties that permit brothels in certain areas and that currently have at least one in business. The number fluctuates, but in recent times twenty-five to thirty brothels have been operating in the state, says George Flint, longtime lobbyist for the Nevada Brothel Owners Association.

That number is a little deceptive, though, because only eight of them can be considered "major brothels," according to Flint. He estimates the eight major brothels do ninety-three percent of the business. The others are mom-and-pop operations in far-flung locales that cater primarily to long-haul truckers.

The eight major brothels are clustered around the tourist destinations of Reno and Las Vegas. The three brothels closest to Las Vegas — two outside Pahrump and one in tiny Crystal — are where the big money is made. Over the past three decades, cab and limo drivers have learned well the route between Las Vegas and Pahrump, escorting high-rolling gamblers, conventioneers, and others to partake of the diverse services the brothels provide.

Legal Tender, Laraine Russo Harper's engrossing tale of her six years as a brothel madam in Pahrump, can be read on three levels. First, the book provides a true insider's look at this fascinating industry. Harper is forthright and detailed in attempting to satisfy the public's seemingly unquenchable curiosity about what happens within a Nevada brothel.

Second, Harper's memoir is heartfelt and highly entertaining. Rest assured, this is no doctoral dissertation on the sex industry. The numerous anecdotes Harper shares from her tenure as a madam run from poignant to hilarious. She is a passionate advocate for the industry but does not ignore its dark side. Above all, the working girls and the customers in this book are not stereotypes. They have human faces and feelings just like the rest of us.

Last but not least, *Legal Tender* has legitimate value for those who want to learn a little something about business management and customer service. Harper brought her wealth of experience in the casino industry to bear on the brothel she managed, with impressive results.

She and the owners worked together to elevate the quality of the brothel experience to a whole new level. You need not be a manager in the sex trade to benefit from her sound advice.

Harper's memoir chronicles a period of dramatic growth and big profits in the brothel business. But times appear to be changing. "The brothel industry is facing the biggest challenge that it's ever been confronted with," Flint says. Actually, the industry is facing two challenges, both of which threaten its long-term survival.

The first is technological. The Internet has opened a new avenue for prostitutes to market themselves. Rather than leaving home for two or three weeks at a stretch to live and work full time in a rural brothel, the women create websites and conduct business without the intermediary of the brothel.

The other challenge is cultural. Society's view of prostitution is simply not as harsh as it once was. Tolerance is gaining the upper hand, allowing prostitutes to work outside the brothels without substantial fear of getting busted. This is certainly true in Las Vegas, where high-priced call girls earn their keep in the suites while hookers sip drinks without hassle at most any casino bar. The risk is higher than it would be in a legal brothel, but understaffed police agencies are so busy chasing killers, thieves, and drug dealers that the illegal sex trade has been pushed to the back burner.

The brothel industry's future may be uncertain, but one thing is undeniable: Prostitution will always be with us. The strongest argument for legalizing prostitution is that it's going to happen anyway, so why not tax and regulate it? It's safer for the working girls and the customers, and the public benefits from the tax revenue.

Despite the logic, it's unlikely that any other state will legalize prostitution in the foreseeable future. Victorian Era notions about sex persist well into the twenty-first century. It's one thing to tolerate low-profile call-girl rings and quite another for voters to endorse the licensing and regulation of brothels. And that means Nevada will continue to be the sole province of legal prostitution — the ultimate manifestation of the live-and-let-live philosophy.

Geoff Schumacher is a Las Vegas journalist and author who grew up in brothel-rich Pahrump, Nevada.

Chapter One

Jersey Girl

Growing up in a small town on the Jersey shore, I never thought I would wind up running a brothel. Hell, I didn't even know brothels existed. Bradley Beach was a summer resort town, a mile square, certainly not big enough to entice a prostitute. The world of prostitution, legal or illegal, was never a thought that crossed my mind.

In 1976 I moved to Las Vegas. It was quite an eye-opening experience leaving a sleepy little beach town and relocating to Sin City. I started working in the casino industry, and that was where I was introduced to the world of prostitution. I worked in gaming for many years, working my way up to executive casino host manager. The goal of every casino host was to keep the high-rollers in the casinos. It didn't take long to learn that big players played big away from the tables, too. They wanted gourmet meals, headliner shows, airfare, limos, suites, and company to share their comps with. As a casino host, I became a provider of all, including the company.

After many years in the gaming industry, I grew tired of the 24/7 gig. For twenty years, I was not home for most of the major holidays. Gamblers wanted to spend the holidays in Vegas and that was my job, hosting the gamblers. A night didn't go by without a series of phone calls from pit bosses, who were usually irate because one of my players was hitting the house hard. I can't recall how many calls I would get, I can only remember that the conversations were all the same.

"Come get your guy off my table, he's killing me!" the pit boss would scream into the phone.

So I would get up, get dressed, and head down to the casino. Oh yeah, he was killing us all right.

"Come on, Dave, I'll buy you dinner," I'd say. "I couldn't sleep and you know I don't like to eat alone."

I ate way too many dinners in the middle of the night and I wasn't even hungry. I was tired! Can't anyone just let me sleep? Not tonight.

After my children were grown, I decided to retire from gaming and the midnight meals. Maybe a more subdued job. Yeah, I liked the sound of that. I decided to go to school and become a manicurist. Set my own schedule, work when I want to, put my heels and elaborate wardrobe in the back of my closet. Perfect!

There I was, sitting at my manicuring table in a beautiful salon, doing nails and shooting the shit all day. I'd wear sundresses and sandals, shorts and T-shirts, and I loved every minute of it. No more fancy outfits and high heels, and no more panty hose! Life was pretty good.

A few months had passed when I ran into an old friend. I hadn't seen him in quite a while and he told me all about a new project he was involved in. He was telling me about this ranch.

"Ranch? When did you become a rancher?" I asked.

He explained that it wasn't your typical ranch, it was a brothel.

"Brothel! How the hell did you get involved with a brothel?"

"I was out golfing and drinking and came across some guy who had a brothel for sale, so I got a group of guys together and we bought it," he said. I think "drinking" was the key word in that sentence!

We talked for a while and at some point during our conversation I realized that this was an interview, not a casual conversation between friends. Laughing, I said, "I'm not your girl. I've been giving it away all my life. What do I know about selling it?"

He tried to persuade me, saying that I would be perfect for the job. Maybe some people would have been offended by that statement, but I considered it a compliment. A few weeks went by and I didn't give it much thought. But my friend, whose name was Sam, called again and suggested I take a ride out to Pahrump and check out his brothel. So I did.

Pahrump is about sixty miles from Las Vegas. I drove west out of town. It was a hot summer day and the desert was in full bloom. The wild burros in Red Rock Canyon looked as if they were totally fed up with the heat, and it was only June. There was a bit of relief from the sweltering temperatures as I drove over the Spring Mountains, about 20 degrees to be exact. Coming down off the mountain I was once again greeted by the desert heat.

The road seemed to go nowhere. Being from the East Coast, where buildings were huddled together, and one town bordered on another, which bordered on another, and so on, I still enjoyed the openness that Nevada had to offer. The drive was actually very scenic and I found myself enjoying the desert solitude. Just me, my cute little convertible, and Toby Keith on the radio; I was perfectly content.

I finally reached Pahrump and turned off the highway. I found myself on yet another road that seemed to go nowhere. Who put these roads here? There's nothing out here, why would you need a road?

At the end of the road I saw a small group of buildings all connected together, sitting in a dirt parking lot. Could this be it? Three double-wide trailers in the middle of nowhere? Reading the sign, I was disappointed to learn that I was in the right place.

Everyone has some preconceived notion of what they think a brothel should look like. Perhaps dark, dirty trailers at the end of a long, lonely road? Well, there was a good reason for that notion, because judging from what I saw in front of me, that's exactly what they were.

Debating whether to turn around and go back to civilization, a part of me said, "What the hell. You're already here, go in. How much worse could it be?"

So I went in. You know how when you think things can't get any worse, they do? Well, they did. I walked into that place and it was so dark and dingy that I wouldn't even put my purse down. There was a good-sized bar straight ahead when you walked in. At the bar were some ladies, and I have to say that in this respect I use the term "ladies" loosely. (No pun intended.) These "ladies" were twice the man my husband would ever be, and he was a strapping, six-foot-four former police officer from New York!

My mind was racing. People pay for this? Are you kidding me? Sam had his partner, Shawn, meet me there to show me around. Shawn is a tall, handsome man with a boyish grin. He introduced himself and said, "You must be Sam's friend." Not an overly perceptive statement, as I was the only woman in the joint who actually looked like a woman. We chatted for a few moments. Shawn seemed like a nice enough guy and tried his best to make me feel welcome. Looking around the place, it was good to see that at least one person besides me had all his teeth.

There were no customers in the place, although that didn't shock me. I couldn't see why anyone in his right mind would want to come to a place like this. The "ladies" looked extremely agitated because a woman had walked through the door, and the bartender seemed irritated because he thought I might want to order a drink. I tried to imagine what would compel Sam to even consider this as a business opportunity. I knew Sam drank, so I could only assume he was drinking when he made this deal. Doesn't my day just keep getting better and better?

I walked with Shawn into the parlor, which was sort of small and wasn't inviting whatsoever. Actually it blended quite nicely with the rest of the place. Covering the floor was blood-red shag carpet that probably hadn't been cleaned since it had been installed twenty years earlier. There were two white pleather — more plastic than leather — couches, three oversized wall sconces with shades, which at one time I'm sure were white, but twenty years of cigarette smoke had taken its toll on them. And there were red velvet drapes, which hung from ceiling to floor and were dirtier than the shades on the sconces, if you could imagine that. There was a chandelier hanging in the middle of the room with crystals that were now opaque from smoke and dirt, but I was sure that at one time it was absolutely beautiful.

This, Shawn explained, is the parlor where we conduct the lineups. Lineups? I'm sure police lineups would be far more attractive than anything here. Okay, no need to spend any more time in this room, I was thinking to myself, I've seen about all that I care to see here.

We proceeded to the rooms where the ladies entertained their clients. They were small and dirty with a double-sized mattress on a plywood platform. No box springs, no bed frames, just a mattress on a sheet of plywood with four makeshift wooden legs. The linens looked a lot like the shades on the sconces in the parlor. They were threadbare, dingy, and stained. There wasn't a piece of furniture in the room that matched, and a shadeless lamp was sitting on the floor next to the bed. I couldn't believe what I was seeing and had an even harder time imagining that anyone would pay for sex with these ladies in a place like this.

It seemed to me that I had been to both ends of the spectrum. At one time I handled high-rollers who would accept nothing less than the best of the best. And now this. Talk about night and day! The more we walked, the worse it got. As Shawn and I toured the property, he must have noticed the look of disbelief on my face. He explained that this was not the brothel he was proposing.

"We have plans to transform this property into a resort," Shawn said.

"Plans . . . this transformation will take more than plans," I answered. "It will take a miracle."

Shawn replied that he thought I was the one person who could pull off that miracle.

I wasn't quite sure where Shawn had gotten his information to think that I could pull off a miracle like that, but I was betting it probably came from Sam, who I was sure was drinking at the time. I knew Sam well enough to know that if he had seen this place when he was not, he never would have considered it an investment opportunity.

I looked at Shawn's plans and I must say they were impressive. What he envisioned was a first-class, upscale destination resort. Restaurant, retail, pool, Jacuzzis, salon, spa — all the amenities you would expect to find at a five-star resort but with a kicker: legal prostitution. My interest was piqued.

I told Shawn that I would have to discuss the possibility with my family. After all, I didn't want to do anything that would embarrass them. I told Shawn that I would get back to him and we left it at that.

On the drive home, my mind was desperately trying to process what I had seen over the last couple of hours. "You can't really be considering working there, could you? You wouldn't really leave that nice, clean, little salon to go there, would you? You're a manicurist, not a madam! Are you crazy?"

Crazy or not, I am a woman of my word. I told Shawn that I would discuss the possibility with my family, and that was what I did.

I first spoke with my husband, who was very supportive. What guy wouldn't be? "I love my wife's job" seemed to be the fitting response.

Next: my very animated daughter. Her first response was, "What are you going to do there? Are you going to . . .?" I interrupted her and told her that I would be running the brothel. I would be the madam.

"Oh, okay, I could see you doing that," she said.

At that point, I began to wonder what it was that I portrayed to other people. Oh well.

Next up was my son. His reaction was totally unexpected. I didn't even finish my sentence when he picked up his cell phone and started dialing. He couldn't dial fast enough. "Hey, you'll never guess what my mom is doing . . . how cool is that?"

So, there you have it. Apparently, the family wouldn't be embarrassed.

I called Shawn and arranged a meeting. "Okay, I'll see you Thursday at two o'clock." Thursday rolled around and Shawn and I met for a cup of coffee.

"So, what's the verdict?" Shawn asked.

"Well, I spoke with my husband and my kids and they don't seem to have a problem with me taking this job." I always knew our family was a bit dysfunctional, but I never realized how dysfunctional we really were. I was considering the job and they didn't have a problem with me taking it. We really are screwed up!

"This is what I can do for you," I said to Shawn. "I will build your brothel, decorate all your interiors, put procedures in place, and have you up and running within a year."

"A year! That's fantastic," he said. "What happens after a year?"

"Well, if I still like you, and you still like me after a year, we'll revisit this whole thing. How does that sound?"

"Sounds like a deal to me." We shook hands and that was that.

As I drove home I couldn't help but think, what have you gotten yourself into? Put procedures in place? You don't know anything about prostitution, so what procedures could you possibly put into place? What procedures could there possibly be for prostitution? How many "procedures" could there be in selling sex? What were you thinking? I found myself arguing with myself. Congratulations, you are now a sex merchant, a retailer of sorts, I guess, yes, a sex retailer, a sex peddler, a seller of sex — a madam.

That was it. I did it. I was a madam. Well, that didn't take long. I guess if I could make the transition into a madam that quickly, I could transform the brothel into a resort. It appeared I was pretty good at this transitioning stuff, so how hard could it be?

I couldn't help thinking back to my early casino days. I was so new and naïve and I didn't know a thing about gaming. The situation I was in now really wasn't that unfamiliar to me. I didn't know a thing about legal prostitution. Well, I certainly understand the concept, but I didn't know anything about the business side of it.

I laughed to myself as I compared my new endeavor with the gaming business. I remembered in the casino industry that "BJ" stood for "blackjack." Not anymore! It had a whole new meaning now. Many things would take on new meanings from that point forward.

Shawn was a hard guy to say no to. Although he was a few years younger than me, it was plain to see that he was an extremely successful businessman. He spoke with such certainty that you just couldn't help but believe in him. And then there was that boyish grin. It was that grin, you know, the grin that makes you drop your guard. The one that doesn't allow you to think straight.

Did I make the right decision? Are you sure you can do this? Again I reminded myself, you didn't know anything about the casino industry when you started working there, so don't sell yourself short. You are your own success story . . . you can do this.

As my friends heard the news that I was now a madam, they were all of the same opinion: "That is the perfect job for you."

What the hell did that mean? Why would people think this would be the perfect job for me? What was it that I did that would lead people to think that?

Okay, I admit I'm not your typical, ordinary, run-of-the-mill person.

I tend to be spontaneous, unpredictable, fun-loving, and unconventional. There wasn't a lot I took too seriously. I think life is too short to take things too seriously. I guess it was evident that I was a very spontaneous person. After all, I just became a madam, right?

Maybe my being voted "Most Likely to Commit a Homicide" in my senior year of high school led my friends to believe this was the perfect job for me. And I was given that honor by the teachers, not the students!

When I was growing up in New Jersey, if your last name ended with two consonants and a vowel, that did it, you had to be connected. Talk about profiling! Maybe their thought process was an "unconventional" job for an "unconventional" person. They may have been right about the job part, but not the homicide part.

I started working with the assumption that what I didn't know about the business, which at that point was everything, Shawn could teach me. I knew Sam didn't know anything about the brothel business. Sam would strike you as the kind of guy who was always looking for the fast track to becoming rich. So my plan was to rely on Shawn.

So much for plans. There is an old Italian saying that translates to, You make plans and God laughs. Well, He was having a party with me!

It turned out Shawn didn't know anything about the brothel business either. He just "happened upon" this particular business that was for sale and thought it might be a fun endeavor. What kind of people would buy a business they knew nothing about? Rich boys and their toys. As it turned out, he was relying on me!

I started researching the brothel business. I pulled all the state statutes and codes that governed the industry. I knew the first step was to learn the laws and regulations, and let me tell you, there were plenty of them. I had never studied for a job before, especially not after I already had the job! Throughout my career as madam, I would reference those books quite frequently.

I dragged my high heels and my elaborate wardrobe out from the back of the closet. They didn't stay there as long as I had planned. Of course, being a madam was something I hadn't planned on either. Really, who would plan on becoming a madam? Young children dream of becoming firemen and policemen and nurses and teachers. Some of those dreams come true through planning. You train or you go to school and get a degree to transform those dreams into reality. But a madam?

There was no training programs or schools for madams. What were the qualifications? What were the requirements? Well, I wasn't a virgin. Maybe that was all the criteria I would need.

The drive from Las Vegas to the middle of nowhere had now become a daily ritual, just me, my cute little convertible, and Toby Keith. If Toby knew where I was driving him to every day, he'd shit! I thought, I have to get some new CDs. I love Toby, but I'm going to need a little variety now that I will be spending so much time on the road. Was I nuts? I used to work right around the corner from my house. Now, I'm driving to another county for a job I don't know a thing about! I didn't have any idea yet that on some days that drive would be the best part of my day.

During my first few weeks at the brothel, I just observed the employees, the ladies, and the few customers who wandered in. They were an interesting bunch. It seemed to be more like The Breakfast Club than a brothel. Customer service did not exist. It appeared that everyone had mistaken hospitality for hostility. Everybody in that place had an attitude. The minute anyone walked in, it seemed that they were a "bother." Gee, I can't imagine why there never was an abundance of customers in the place. It wasn't bad enough that the place looked so awful, they had to treat people that way, too?

The ladies were rude, crude, and tough. Hardly the traits that a guy would desire, much less pay for. Their language was vulgar, so much so that even a sailor would blush. Really, the only way I could confirm

that they were indeed women was through the results of their STD/
HIV tests; they really did possess female genitalia.

I quickly learned my way around the property. At first I was hesitant
to wander too far from my office into the maze of narrow hallways con-
necting one trailer to another. I couldn't be sure what may have been
lurking in those dark, dingy hallways. The bar and parlor were in one
trailer, the ladies' rooms were in another, and the third trailer was the
kitchen/dining room and lounge area for the ladies.

The kitchen was just like a kitchen you would find in any manufactured home. It wasn't a commercial kitchen. Naturally, the kitchen was
modeled in the same décor as the rest of the place: filth. Everything
was dirty and covered in grease. How anyone could prepare a meal
in that filth was beyond me. There was an oven in the kitchen that
went from zero degrees to 400 degrees and nothing in between. The
cook made breakfast and dinner for the ladies. If you didn't like what
she cooked, you didn't eat. It was that simple. All the ladies ate at the
large dining room table, labeled "the training table." There they shared
stories about the daily dramas that were going on in their lives. They
would complain about their "man," which translated to "pimp." After
all these years, that was something I just could not comprehend. Why
on Earth would you give your money to a pimp when you are working
in a legal house of prostitution? It didn't make any sense then and it
doesn't make any sense now. I was surprised at how many ladies had
pimps, then and now.

When there were no customers in the brothel, which was most of
the time, the ladies would sit around and watch TV. That always made
things interesting. You see, there was no cable at the brothel. Who was
going to run cable to the middle of nowhere? There was a satellite dish,
but only one box, so the ladies had to agree on what they were going to
watch. Agree? Are you crazy? There were always catfights. They would
sit and argue on the old, tattered brown couch and loveseat. I never did

know if that furniture was brown originally, or just became that color from the grit and grime over the years. It was apparent everywhere you looked that cleanliness was not a priority at this brothel. There was a housekeeper at the brothel, but I couldn't figure out what she might have cleaned.

An average day consisted of fourteen to sixteen hours, not including the sixty-mile drive each way. I would shower for what seemed to be hours, trying desperately to cleanse myself of the filth that surrounded me during the day.

As time passed and I made my observations, it was clear that the majority of the staff had to go, not to mention the ladies. Housekeeping would be the first plan of action. I went in to the housekeeping office and there was a housekeeper, sitting behind the desk smoking a joint. Well, this was going to be easier than I thought. I fired her right on the spot. The ladies were quite upset when they heard that I had fired a housekeeper. Apparently "housekeeper" was just a title. What she really did for a living was sell marijuana to the ladies. I had fired their connection. Well, I guess that explained why she never cleaned anything. She didn't have time. The drug-dealing business can be so demanding. I hired new housekeepers and made cleanliness a priority. What a concept!

The bar was next. All the bartenders were male, and since they weren't swamped with customers, they entertained themselves by fondling the ladies. They would grab and grope them, stick their hands down their shirts and up their skirts. They were all over the ladies. When a policy was put in effect to stop that behavior, the bartenders could find no reason to stay. Another problem solved. The bartenders hired from that point forward were all females.

After the old bartenders left, the ladies felt as though I cared about their well-being. They began to open up to me with stories about the previous ownership and how a manager, who was a man approaching his golden years, would force them to sleep with him. Evidently, he had a room at the brothel and stayed on the property quite often. He wasn't what you would consider an attractive man. He was short and stocky and walked around in leopard print boxers with a matching robe. Picture that, a short, stocky senior citizen strutting around in his leopard print boxers, with his stomach hanging over, as if he's some kind of king or something. Hey, King, have you taken a good look at your kingdom? Are you kidding me? They said he was pompous, arrogant, and demanding, not to mention a self-proclaimed "ladies' man." Oh, I'm sure he was a vision to feast your eyes on. He apparently drank quite a bit and the way the ladies would tell the story, he was much worse when he was drinking. I've never known alcohol to enhance anyone's personality, and apparently it didn't enhance his. The ladies, in fear of losing their jobs, would comply with all his demands.

In the years to come, I would learn that this was quite a common practice in the brothel industry. Owners, who were primarily men, would force the ladies to have sex with them routinely. I guess it was one of the "perks," but it was something I never agreed with. The ladies are still people, and by the way, you idiot, they make you a lot of money. Don't you think you should treat them better? If it weren't for the ladies, you would be out of business, moron! I am sorry to say this type of activity still takes place today.

The shift managers worked in the office area and were responsible for booking any parties that the ladies may have during their shifts. A "party" is the term used for a session or sexual experience between the customer and the lady of his or her choice. The ladies are independent contractors who negotiate their own prices. The house (the brothel) does not get involved whatsoever in any pricing that the ladies quote. The house does set "minimums" for the use of certain "party rooms," and there is also a house minimum. The house minimum at this particular brothel was two hundred dollars. Every house set its own minimums. If a customer came in with less than the house minimum, he wouldn't be able to party with a lady.

The lady would escort the customer to her room and then the negotiation would begin, with the lady asking what type of activity the customer might be interested in. The lady would then quote the customer a price. Some customers agreed right away. Others did not, and at that point the lady and the customer would negotiate until price and activities were agreed upon. The customer would pay the lady before any services were rendered. The lady would bring the payment — cash, credit card, travelers' checks, etc. — to the shift manager. The shift manager would process the transaction. In watching the shift managers, I soon learned that they had a license to steal. There was no accountability for anything.

There was one shift manager who had a franchise going with one of the ladies. They partnered up and had their own business within the walls of the brothel. The lady would not book the party, but rather give the shift manager a percentage and keep the rest of the money for herself. "Booking" a party consisted of, at the time, recording the lady's name and the amount of the party on a log sheet. The shift manager would then place the money in the cash drawer. But with this particular shift manager and lady, nothing was going to the house because nothing was being recorded. It was like the old Vegas soft-count rooms where they counted the money drops from the gaming tables: one for you, two for me. There was a 50/50 split between the lady and the house; that is, with the exception of this one enterprising shift manager.

Other shift managers were in cahoots with the bartenders, who would get the ladies drunk. When a lady came up to the office to book a party, the shift managers would skim money off the top and put it in their pockets. The lady was too drunk to notice. The shift manager would give the bartender a "kickback" for his help. Nothing like teamwork!

As for the maintenance man, now there was a piece of work! The guy couldn't fix anything. Whatever he worked on was destroyed by the time he was finished with it. Then you would have to call in a professional. So, we're paying someone to fix all the stuff that he breaks? That makes sense! Perhaps if he were sober, he could have fixed something, but I wouldn't bet on it.

I would walk around the property thinking that I was on the Island of Misfit Toys. Where did all these people come from? But more importantly, why were they all here?

The weeding-out process took some time, because even brothels had to comply with labor laws. Red lights and red tape — what a combination.

Chapter Two

THE GHOST OF MADAMS PAST

Shortly after I took the plunge into the world of legal prostitution, I began to learn of "the ghost." I don't know why I was surprised to learn that most of the ladies, as well as the staff, believed the ghost of the previous madam still loomed within those walls. I began to think this place was worse than working for the mob. Death was the only way out of the mob, but here, well, even death didn't get you out. What had I gotten myself into?

There were ladies who refused to stay in certain rooms because at one time the room belonged to the ghost. There were reports of the ghost seen roaming the hallways at night in search of something. What it was looking for, no one was really sure. I can remember ladies running out of their rooms, screaming at the top of their lungs and frantically seeking some type of safety net, which happened to be me. Trying to catch their breath, with tears streaming down their faces, they would tell me they heard footsteps and doors slamming. They were terrified. "I know it was her," they would say, trembling. These were grown women.

The ghost's activities seemed more prominent after dark. However, on occasion some ladies had caught glimpses of her turning corners or entering a room during the day. I came to learn that the ladies, like gamblers, are very superstitious.

The ghost was seen by one lady at a time. She never made her presence known when there were two or more ladies to witness her. It didn't take long, though, after a lady reported seeing the ghost, that the rest of the ladies in the house were in an uproar. In an instant there would be a house full of frightened women, crying and clamoring for safety. They were all equally upset so, at times, it took a minute to determine which one actually had seen the ghost.

One time I heard a blood-curdling scream. I took off running down the hallway but in a flash I found myself flat on my back, sprawled on the floor with a hysterical lady on top of me. What the hell?

"She's here, she's here!"

That's all that she said, over and over, for about five minutes.

"What does she want?" she cried.

I thought to myself that if that ghost was sharing the same thought process I was at that time, she wants to get the hell out of here.

"Sandy, calm down. I'm here, it's okay."

I sat on the floor in the hallway holding Sandy for about fifteen minutes until she calmed down.

"Are you okay?"

"I think so."

I took Sandy back to her room. She curled up in her bed in the fetal position and I held her and rocked her until she fell asleep. As she was sleeping I couldn't help but look at her. She looked like such a child, but Sandy was in her mid-thirties.

Some of the ladies enjoyed seeing the ghost. Hattie, a lady who was very spiritual, was one of the few who enjoyed seeing her. Hattie would come running to my office, all excited, shouting, "I just saw her. She was going into the dining room. You should have seen it, it was awesome!"

"Saw who?"

"Jane, the ghost, of course."

Of course, what was I thinking? Hattie was on a first-name basis with the ghost. Hattie went on to say, "I even spoke to her."

"Really, what did she say?"

"Well, she didn't answer me, but I kept on talking to her."

What a shock. A lot of the ladies didn't answer Hattie, but that never stopped Hattie from carrying on a conversation anyway. I told Hattie that should she have the opportunity to speak to the ghost again, please inform her that if she plans on staying here, she has to pay rent just like everyone else.

The ladies paid daily rent for their room and board. That included their private room, housekeeping services, and their food. Hattie, who was a little different, to say the least, said, "Okay" and sauntered off. I'm sure they're all like her — on her planet.

Some of the ladies would hold séances and try to reach out to Jane. That would freak the other ladies out. They would sit in a circle, holding hands, and call out her name. "Jane, are you there? Can you hear me? Jane, please show your presence." This would go on for quite some time. Jane never appeared.

The tales of Jane were handed down from lady to lady. This, apparently, had been going on for years. No one who was currently at the brothel had ever worked with Jane. They just heard stories about her walking the hallways, appearing at her will, making noises, slamming doors, laughing. You know, all the things that ghosts do.

As new ladies came to work at the brothel, they were all brought up to date on the latest Jane sightings. Misery loves company. The new ladies listened wide-eyed to the tales of Jane, hanging on every word.

"What does she look like?" Now, here is where it got interesting, because who was telling the story determined how Jane looked. The "senior" ladies who were attesting to the fact of the sightings now inter-jected their take on what Jane looked like. Jane was many things to many people, apparently. She was tall and slender, short and stocky, long gray hair, short gray hair. Hell, she was even a blonde! If the ladies couldn't agree on a TV show to watch, you really didn't expect them to agree on the ghost, did you? It wouldn't take long before a full-blown argument ensued about what Jane looked like. I would have to run out of my office to break it up before things got out of hand.

"Ladies, knock it off. Don't even tell me you're fighting over the ghost!"

Then they would all start telling me that they "know" what Jane looks like. "I've seen her, I know what she looks like." Here we go all over again.

"Okay, ladies, let me tell you what I know. I can settle this once and for all. How about I just move your stuff into Jane's old room and then you can get a real good look at her one more time, just to be sure?" That ended the argument real fast. No one wanted Jane's room, except for Hattie, of course.

The staff had a different take on Jane. When things were missing, Jane took them. When reports were to be put in my box, they would respond, "I put it in your box. Jane probably took it out." When things were left in places where they shouldn't have been, it was, that's right, Jane. To the staff, Jane was a matter of convenience, the perfect scapegoat. I learned that one of the rooms had never been cleaned, because the housekeeper was told, by Jane, to stay out of there. "This is my room," Jane informed the housekeeper. There was no doubt in my mind that she was smoking weed at the time. The housekeeper, not Jane. As far as I knew, Jane didn't do drugs. I did hear that she liked her liquor, though. I could relate to that. In the thirty-odd years that I have been in the work force, I never drank on the job. But this place . . . I was starting to consider it!

Even the few regular customers who visited the bar knew of Jane. They would tell stories of how the brothels were the only thing she knew. She was a former working girl who, after her youth had passed and she could no longer command the price for her services, became a madam. No one was really sure if Jane had worked at this brothel as a working girl, but they knew she was the madam here. That seemed to be the consensus among the ladies, the staff, and the customers alike.

When the customers were sober, they admitted to never actually having seen Jane, but after a few drinks, Jane and them went way back. They would tell stories of sitting at the bar and drinking with Jane. The story would go something like this. "Yeah, I remember a few years back, I was sitting right here at this bar, on this very same barstool. The barkeep was sitting on a stool, right over there behind the bar, head down, asleep, I think. Yeah, he was sleeping. I was sitting here all alone, minding my own business, when lo and behold, there she was. Jane, right in front of my own eyes! She sat on the stool right next to me. Right there, where you're sitting now. She said, 'You mind?' and took my whiskey and drank it down. Can you believe that? Oh yeah, Jane loved her whiskey." And they would go on and on about how Jane would tell them stories of the old times.

Jane's death was a mystery, much like her life. There were as many different stories of her disappearance as there were of her appearance. Supposedly she died at the brothel. It was rumored that she was murdered by an old "trick" who had fallen in love with her when she was a younger "working girl." A "trick" was how the ladies referred to their customers. Not in their presence, of course. Jane's trick spent tens of thousands of dollars with her and later on, in his older years, grew bitter and came back and killed her. Now, who was telling the story determined how she was killed.

"Shot her in cold blood," one would say.

"No, she was stabbed to death, forty-seven times."

"No, she wasn't stabbed, she was strangled. Dragged down that hallway right there and strangled. Yup, he strangled her with his bare hands, kissed her on the forehead and walked out. No one ever did see him again."

Some would even venture to say that Jane took her own life. "She wasn't' murdered, she hung herself. She couldn't bear not being a working girl anymore. Couldn't stand the thought that she wasn't good enough to pay for anymore, so she hung herself."

Everybody seemed to have a different Jane story. They all would agree on one thing, though: Jane would never leave the brothel. The brothel was the only thing she had ever known. The brothel was her home. The brothel was her life. Jane was there to stay.

Great. Out of all the brothels in Nevada, I worked at the one with a ghost! You can rest assured that when I leave this place, I'm taking my ghost with me.

As if the ghost stories were not enough, I was working at the brothel for about six months when I was served with a summons to appear in court to testify in an attempted murder case.

Attempted murder? I have come to realize that if it weren't for bad luck, I wouldn't have any luck at all. You see, we had a limo driver working for us. His name was Tom. Tom was a strange fellow, but blended well with the rest of the crew. In addition to bringing customers to the brothel, Tom would bring the ladies to the brothel when they were scheduled to arrive. Tom was not only a limo driver, but an enterprising individual, as I later learned.

Tom had developed relationships with some of the ladies he brought to the brothel on a regular basis. One relationship in particular didn't work out too well for Tom. It seemed that he and Janet, one of the regularly scheduled ladies, developed a business relationship they thought would be lucrative for both of them. You can't blame someone for trying to make an extra buck, right? After many lengthy business meetings between

Tom and Janet, it was decided that Tom would front the money for the merchandise they had planned to resell for a profit. Buy wholesale, sell retail. Thousands of Americans make their living this way, so why not Tom and Janet? A handshake consummated the deal.

Tom went to Las Vegas and secured the merchandise, solely encumbering the out-of-pocket expenses, just as they agreed. Tom then delivered the merchandise to Janet's house. According to the plan, once he delivered the merchandise, he would be reimbursed by Janet for his expenses, just as they agreed. Keep in mind that all the securing of and delivering of merchandise was taking place by using the company limousine. Well, any smart businessman would tell you that it was best to keep your overhead as minimal as possible. Why use your own gas and your own car when you have access to the company gas card and the company car?

Upon Tom's arrival, he was greeted at the door by Janet. He walked into Janet's house to find two men waiting for him as well. By the way, the merchandise that Tom had secured and they planned to sell was cocaine.

Okay, so the two men took the cocaine from Tom and then proceeded to beat the hell out of him. They beat him with a lead pipe and kicked him until he lay in a lifeless heap on Janet's floor as Janet stood by and witnessed the whole ordeal. They taped Tom's mouth, hands and ankles with duct tape and threw him into the back of their car. All three of them drove well into the night to find just the right location to dump him. There it was, out in the desert of a neighboring state.

The three of them dragged Tom across the desert and buried the lifeless heap in a shallow — very shallow — grave. They swept away their footprints and got back in the car. They went back to Janet's house. Now they have to get rid of the limousine, right? They drove the limousine way out of town and abandoned it.

Tom, however, wasn't dead. About four hours after he was dumped in the desert he regained consciousness, broke free of the tape, and managed to crawl to a highway. Covered in blood from head to toe, a trucker spotted him, picked him up, and took him to a hospital. There, he told his story. Naturally, the police were notified. Broken bones, cracked skull, contusions over ninety percent of his body, face swollen beyond recognition — Tom was a mess.

Since Tom was an employee of the brothel and Janet was an independent contractor who also worked at the brothel, that's how I became involved. I was summoned to testify as to the character of both Tom and Janet, and, of course, was questioned as to any knowledge I may have had about their dope deal and everything that occurred thereafter.

Can you believe it? The only time I had even set foot in a courtroom before was for my divorce, umpteen years ago.

"Do you solemnly swear to tell the truth, the whole truth, and nothing but the truth, so help you God?"

"Yes."

"Can you please tell the court what you know about the people you see sitting at that table in this courtroom today?"

"Yes, they're nuts!"

Funny, I didn't remember anything like this being discussed in the job interview. Who would have thought selling sex would be so complicated! It seemed really simple at the time. What a great job; no inventory problems. You sell it and you still got it. How hard could it be?

Needless to say, Tom was terminated from the company. Janet was found guilty and sentenced to two years in prison on conspiracy charges. The other two guys were found guilty and sentenced to five years in prison on attempted murder charges.

Chapter Three

Brothel Management 101

Construction had begun on what was to become the resort. New personnel were in place and new ladies were beginning to appear at the brothel. The ladies were booked in through another office, which wasn't located at the brothel. Now, don't get me wrong. They weren't a higher caliber of ladies, they were just new. Every week the lineup would change. You see, ladies would book into the brothel for a minimum of two weeks. They lived at the brothel while they were working at the brothel. The county codes that regulate the brothels in Southern Nevada stipulate that the ladies cannot leave the brothel during the time frame that they are contracted to work, other than for a few hours, once a week, to take care of their banking needs when they got paid or what have you. The codes in Northern Nevada were different. Up north, the ladies could leave the brothel every night and return the next day.

Since every lady at the brothel didn't book in for the same two weeks, each week the lineup would change. There were always ladies departing and ladies arriving. Each week was, to say the least, full of suspense, as

I never knew who would show up on the doorstep.

I remember one day I was at the shift manager's station and a woman came up to the desk. I asked, "Can I help you?"

She said, "Yes, I am here to work."

I asked her if she was applying for a housekeeper or cook position. She informed me that she was a working girl. Unable to gather my control quick enough, the words just rolled off my tongue, "You're joking."

"No, I'm Fantasy."

Fantasy? This girl was a nightmare!

I called the booking office and asked for the photos that Fantasy had submitted for employment. I looked at the photos. I looked at the lady standing at the counter. I looked at the photos again. I looked at the lady standing at the counter again. You've got to be kidding me. Her photos were actually quite nice, but the girl at the counter could scare a bulldog off a meat truck!

Okay, gain your composure and go out there and say something to her, but you know she can't stay. All right, I'm going to diplomatically throw her out. Got it.

"Sweetheart, when were these photos taken?"

"Oh, those . . . they were probably taken ten, maybe fifteen years ago."

"I see. Well, here's the thing. You see, when you submit photos for employment, we really need you to look like your photos. Do you think you look like these photos?"

"Well, I may have gained a few pounds, but other than that, yes, that's me all right."

This wasn't going well. Apparently, fifteen years later, her eyes weren't what they used to be either.

"Okay. Fantasy, I am terribly sorry, honey, but apparently the office that booked you in inadvertently booked you for the wrong week. You see, we do not have any room for you this week, sweetheart."

"Oh, well, you know, I don't know when I will be able to book back in. My schedule is quite full and I actually managed to squeeze YOU into MY schedule."

"I understand, honey, and believe me, it is certainly our loss."

As Fantasy was leaving, she yelled over her shoulder, "Well, I don't know when you'll hear from me again. I'm very busy."

I was thinking to myself: "Never works for me." As luck would have it, I never did hear from her again.

Tattoos were an up-and-coming thing for girls in those days and we were getting a lot of ladies at the brothel with numerous tattoos. I called over to the booking office and inquired about whether they asked how many tattoos a lady had. No, of course not. I informed them that they should start asking about tattoos, as some of the ladies who were showing up at the brothel had so many tattoos they looked like comic books.

To my surprise, one week we had a lady arrive at the brothel who actually looked quite nice. Now we were getting somewhere. She checked in to her room and settled in. The next day we received the fax that indicated her STD/HIV tests had cleared through the clinic, so off she went to the Sheriff's Department for her sheriff's card. All brothel workers, whether they are company employees or independent contractors, must have a valid sheriff's card. The Sheriff's Department performs a background check on each employee and independent contractor, as well as taking fingerprints, which are run through their database. Coming back with her sheriff's card in hand, which proudly displayed "licensed prostitute" across the front, she was ready for the floor. She went off to her room to change.

The ladies could wear lingerie, bikinis, bra and panty sets, club wear, anything that worked for them as long as it was sexy. We were all excited to see her "floor ready" as she was a pretty girl. That was quite a new concept for this brothel. As luck would have it, the shift manager was calling for a lineup. We had a guy on the couch in the parlor and we had eight ladies in the house. I went through the back hallway and sneaked to the back of the parlor to watch the lineup.

If you wanted the "traditional" brothel experience, you would ask for a lineup. Red lights — yes, just like the old cherries you would see on police cars in the 1970s — were strategically placed throughout the property to notify the ladies that we were having a lineup. When the ladies saw the red lights turned on, they would gravitate toward the hallways on either side of the parlor. What brothel wouldn't have red lights? That was a must. A brothel without red lights would be like a casino without slot machines.

We would make an announcement over the PA system, "Ladies, we have a lineup. Ladies, we have a lineup, please." That announcement was for a "regular" lineup. A "regular" lineup consisted of a single male on the couch. There were different codes for different types of lineups. "Ladies, we have a lineup in the parlor. Ladies, we have a lineup in the parlor, please" indicated that there was a black gentleman on the couch. It wasn't a racial thing. You see, a lot of the ladies had black pimps who would forbid them to offer their services to another black man in fear that he might try to entice their "woman" to work for them.

Why on Earth would anyone in a brothel have a pimp? Does that make sense to you? It made no sense to me why a lady would give all her money to some guy who might beat the shit out of her if she didn't earn enough money. We used to keep theatrical makeup on hand because it wasn't unusual for a lady to show up at the brothel with black eyes, busted lips, and bruises all over. I couldn't put them in the lineup looking like that, but if I didn't let them work, their pimps would beat them again for not making any money. So, I would cover up their bruises with makeup so they could work.

The world of pimps was a whole different world. Most pimps had more than one woman working for them. They would all reside together in the same household, which the women paid for, naturally. Women who belonged to the same pimp were "wife-in-laws" to one another. If one woman wasn't making her share of the money or got into an argument with another wife-in-law, the pimp would order the other wife-in-laws to beat her. That was how the pimp maintained order among the wife-in-laws.

There was a pecking order as well. The wife-in-law who earned the most money or had been with her pimp the longest, or both, was labeled the "bottom bitch." The only one who could beat the bottom bitch was her pimp. It just goes to show that every entity has its status!

It never ceased to amaze me how or why those women believed, without a doubt, that their pimp loved them. "Look in the mirror. You have two black eyes. How could someone who loves you do something like that?"

"He beats me BECAUSE he loves me."

And there was nothing you could say to change their minds. They were brainwashed. They lived in fear.

Some ladies who began working at the brothel realized they didn't need a pimp anymore and managed to break away. Others didn't know any different way of life and chose to stay. I suppose it was more or less like being in an abusive marriage. Some battered wives flee and yet so many others stay. To each her own, I guess, but many of them were kids. Where were their families? Where were their mothers?

Because of pimps, not all the ladies offered their services to black men. The ladies did have choices as to who they would offer their services to. Their choices consisted of black, single women, couples and disabled clients. The call for a couples lineup was, "Ladies we have a couples lineup. Ladies, we have a couples lineup, please." The "regular" call for a lineup was used for a disabled customer. Once the ladies gathered in the hallways, we would let them know that the customer was disabled, physically or mentally. The ladies who did not offer their services to disabled clients would retreat from the hallway. A large portion of brothel clientele was disabled but it took a very special lady to offer her services to disabled clients.

When we, as a society, see disabled children, our hearts go out to them. But those children grow up to become adults and often become the "throwaways" of our society. It is human nature to gravitate toward things that are small and cute. You see it all the time with puppies and kittens. Oh, some of us just love them when they are small, but then they grow and don't seem so cute anymore. Now they are destroying the furniture, barking, and doing all the things that dogs and cats do. How many abandoned animals have you seen? You don't see too many abandoned puppies or kittens, do you?

Disabled people have the same desires and needs as those of us who are more fortunate. They crave sex, too! I am proud to say that most of my ladies offered their services to those who were disabled.

A lot of customers were new to the brothel scene and were uncomfortable having a lineup. We offered an alternative. A customer who did not want a lineup could go to the bar and have cocktails with the ladies, shoot a game of pool, and get to know them on a one-on-one basis. A customer could pick a lady from the bar if he so desired, and the lady would escort him back to her room to negotiate a party.

Okay, now let's get back to the lineup at hand. "Ladies from the right. Ladies from the left," the shift manager called. The ladies entered from either side of the parlor and lined up right in front of the customer sitting on the couch. They introduced themselves, one at a time, to the customer. The only thing the ladies were permitted to say during a lineup was their name. Anything else would be considered dirty hustling and we'll get to that later.

After all the introductions were made, the customer would be asked to pick the lady (or ladies) of his choice. I was watching like a proud mother hen because I actually had a lady in the lineup who was pretty! How often had that happened? Oh, never. This was exciting.

And then here she comes. Can't I catch a break? I went to my phone and called the booking office. "You know that pretty girl you booked in this week?"

"Yeah, she's a doll."

"Did you ask about tattoos like I suggested?"

"Oh yes, she only has one."

"That is correct. Did you happen to ask about the ONE tattoo that she has?"

"No."

"It is a dragon."

"So? A dragon isn't anything offensive."

"No, it isn't, but this dragon's tail starts at her left ankle, the dragon's body goes up her entire left leg, across her back and the head wraps around her neck."

The whole left side of her body was a tattoo. And let me tell you something, this dragon was no "Puff." This dragon had an attitude, breathing fire. There were flames all over her! It was at this point that I learned I needed to be very specific.

By the way, our little dragon-lady did not get picked out of the lineup. Gee, I wonder why?

Having made all the adjustments to the tattoo issue, things began to fall into place. That is, until piercing became all the rage. We had a lady show up at the brothel with so many face piercings that I just knew if she took a drink of water, she would look like the fountains at the Bellagio Hotel in Las Vegas.

What would compel anyone to put holes in her face? What goes through her mind? I remember going berserk when my daughter had her tongue pierced. It goes to show, things could always be worse. And this was definitely worse. The process of booking the ladies in from another location happened for about a year until it was moved to the brothel. From that point forward, I hired all the ladies.

Hiring the ladies was strategic. Before, I would just wind up with whoever the other office happened to book. When I took over the hiring, there was a plan. Variety is the spice of life. Our lineups must have variety. We must always have an assortment of blondes, brunettes, redheads, short hair, long hair, petite builds, tall ladies, short ladies, huge breasts, not-so-huge breasts, Asian, black, Caucasian, blue eyes, brown eyes, green eyes. We had to have a wide selection in order to capitalize on every man's wishes. I started a database of all the ladies I booked listing all their pertinent information.

As time progressed, I learned more and more about the industry. Every day I learned something. I incorporated what I was learning into the development of the new building. If nothing else, this chapter in my life proved to be a learning experience that no length of time will allow me to forget.

You remember the blood-red shag carpet I told you about in the old brothel? Well, that carpet was installed just like any other carpet would be installed: over a foundation, with a pad and then the carpet — you know, standard installation. The ladies were very creative. You must remember that they were more or less like prisoners. They had nothing but time on their hands when they were not entertaining a client. They could not leave the brothel, so they found ways to beat the system.

The carpet installation aided them in one of those ways. They would take a razor blade and make slits in the carpet. Now they had a place to stash drugs or money they were withholding from the house. In the new building, there would be no padding installed. The carpet would be glued directly to the foundation. Now I wouldn't have that to worry about. But give them time, they will come up with something else. They always did.

I was busy putting new procedures in place that would be implemented when we moved the ladies to the new building. For example, I implemented "shakedowns," which would be conducted by security.

Randomly, security would perform a shakedown, or search, of a lady's room. Security was to look for any money or drugs that a lady might be hiding. A "zero tolerance" program for drugs was put into effect. I did not want to rehabilitate anyone or counsel them on drugs or even change their lifestyle. It was their business if they did drugs, not mine. But just don't do them at the brothel or bring them on the property. What people do on their own time is their own business. But drugs at the brothel, that could jeopardize the license, and as I learned years ago in the gaming business: ALWAYS PROTECT THE LICENSE.

I put together a checklist of everything in the room that should be inspected. The "shakedown checklist" was quite extensive. Outlets and switch plates were unscrewed to inspect behind them; mattresses were lifted, as were the box springs; pictures were removed from the walls. Lotion, shampoo, and conditioner bottles were inspected, as ladies would put either drugs or money in condoms and then place the condoms in their lotion, shampoo, or conditioner. The battery compartments of the ladies' vibrators were checked. I told you they were creative! Air-conditioning filters were removed and inspected. Naturally security checked all their personal belongings: cosmetics, luggage, purses, etc. All their clothing was checked, all pockets were inspected. Padded bras were a popular place to hide things. The ladies would cut slits in the padding and then slip cash or drugs or both in there. Pillows, cushions — you name it and it was a possible hiding place.

The most popular hiding place was on the ladies themselves. Putting money or dugs in a condom and inserting the condom into their vaginas was a foolproof hiding place. We didn't conduct cavity checks, so the next best thing was to conduct a shakedown immediately following a party. Usually they didn't put the condom back in until they showered, so we would shake down their rooms when they were walking their customer out. It was quite a lengthy process that required strategic planning on our part.

In an effort to discourage us from performing shakedowns, the ladies would bring tons of luggage containing clothing, CDs, DVDs, basically everything they owned, so I implemented yet another policy limiting the ladies to two pieces of luggage and a cosmetic bag. It was like a chess game . . . just waiting until the next move.

Of course, shakedowns and other procedures were all done with the ladies' full knowledge. When new procedures were put in place, new forms were created that the ladies would sign when they arrived. In addition to their independent contractor's agreement, they would now sign acknowledgement forms for shakedowns and other policies.

Chapter Four

Movin' On Up

With construction of the new brothel well under way, the lineups were looking good. Once the new building opened, we would be able to house up to twenty-five ladies. Each lady would have her own private suite, private bathroom, walk-in closet, beds that had mattresses, box springs, AND a frame complete with headboard and footboard. There would be new furniture, linens, and towels, plus a commercial laundry facility to clean and disinfect everything. Not only would the new building house twenty-five ladies, but there would be rooms with Jacuzzi tubs and other "specialty" rooms to party in. This was going to be great.

With the new specialty rooms came house minimum prices for those rooms. The brothel did not charge a "room charge." The minimum for a specialty room included the services of the lady. Let's say a Jacuzzi Room had a $1,000 minimum. What that meant was if the customer agreed to pay $1,000 or more for a party, the Jacuzzi Room could be used if they so desired.

The Jacuzzis were considered "public pools," so no sexual activity was permitted in them. It was a great place for foreplay and intimate conversation, but no sexual activity. After relaxing in the Jacuzzi, the lady and her customer would go back to the lady's room for any sexual activity they had negotiated.

The ladies and the staff were very excited about the new developments they saw taking place at the brothel. There was so much construction — everywhere you looked, something was being built.

We never closed the brothel during construction. That made things interesting from time to time. Business was picking up a little as word got out about all the building that was taking place. Each week our website was updated with the construction progress.

The ladies complained endlessly about the noise. Construction workers would show up early in the morning and begin hammering and sawing. The ladies would be awakened at six o'clock every morning and, believe me, they weren't happy about it. Hell, sometimes they didn't go to bed until four or five o'clock in the morning. The construction really took its toll on them.

The ladies had to be available at all hours for a customer who could come in at any time. We were a 24/7 operation. If someone came in at three o'clock in the morning and wanted a lineup, we would wake up all the ladies.

The ladies had three minutes to get ready for a lineup. Just enough time to throw on something sexy, freshen up their makeup, and comb their hair. They all slept in their makeup. You just can't put makeup on in three minutes.

Prostitution is a lucrative business for the ladies, but they work hard for their money. It is a very difficult job. They are "on call," so to speak, twenty-four hours a day when they are at the brothel. They leave their homes, their families, and their pets for two or three weeks at a time. They have to handle the same day-to-day problems that we all encounter, only they have to deal with those problems long distance.

Many of the ladies are married; some have children. Their child skips school and the school calls Mom. We've all been through it. But they can't just leave and go take care of the problem. That tends to make things a bit more difficult. A lot of the ladies are single moms and their families don't know what they do for a living. That makes things even more difficult. And I don't have to tell you how moody women can be from time to time, especially during their time of the month. Believe me, the construction noise did not enhance their personalities!

After months and months of construction, the day everyone was waiting for had finally arrived: moving day. Everyone was so excited. Follow me, ladies, we're movin' on up!

And move up we did. The new place was gorgeous. Now THIS was a brothel. It was so big and there was so much space. No more narrow hallways. The new ones were six feet wide. There were large picture windows all the way down the hallways overlooking the courtyard. The sunlight that flooded the hallways was a welcome sight. In the old brothel, there were no windows in those dark, drab hallways. You felt like you were encased in a tomb. It was very creepy. But this was magnificent! You could walk through the hallway and see the beautiful mountains across the desert. And the courtyard, the pool, the paths . . . how aesthetically appealing they were. The view was breathtaking. I couldn't wait until winter when the snow would blanket the mountaintops.

With the new building came some new procedures. The lineup was lacking something, but what? The ladies would file in, single file from each side of the parlor, meet in the middle, turn and face the customer on the couch and one by one say their names. Boring! It needed pizzazz; it needed movement; it needed to be different.

During the construction phase, two friends of a friend of mine were helping with the final touches. These two guys, a gay couple, Denny and Kenny, had been in the entertainment business a few years back.

Denny was a singer and dancer in one of the production shows at a major hotel on the Las Vegas Strip.

"Denny, do you think you could help me liven up our lineup?" I asked.

"Oh my God, yes," he replied. "It does need something, doesn't it? You get the girls and I'll get Kenny."

"Girls, girls, listen up," Denny said. Denny kind of sung when he spoke. Having a conversation with Denny was like being in a musical. "We're going to have some fun and put a little bit of showbiz glitz into the lineup. Doesn't that sound like fun?"

The ladies all loved Denny and Kenny. I don't know what it was about gay guys, but the ladies loved them.

Denny was in his glory. He thought he was back on the stage, in the limelight, and he loved it. "Okay, girls, now line up like you normally would do." Denny watched them as they filed in to the parlor. "Okay, stop right there. Now, the last girl on the right, I want you to walk up, very sexy, and stand in front of the couch, curtsy, say your name, pivot, and turn and cross over to the lineup and you will now be the last girl on the left side. Now, sweetheart on the left, as she is walking toward you, you start walking toward the couch, curtsy, pivot, and turn and cross over to the right. Then the second girl on the right crosses over and becomes the second girl on the left and so on and so on. Got it? Here, let me show you."

They rehearsed the new lineup routine over and over. Denny, Kenny, and the ladies were having a ball. Denny and Kenny were teaching the ladies how to curtsy and pivot. Kenny was performing the lineup with the ladies as Denny was busy choreographing every step. It took the better part of an afternoon, but they got it.

Denny, who was a stage lighting technician, decided that the track lights illuminating the lineup needed colored gels over them to enhance the ladies' appearances. "I have some in my car. I'll be right back," Denny said. He was so excited as he scampered out the door. Denny came in with gels in an array of colors. Denny experimented with the different colors until he found just the right combinations. "Perfect. Now isn't that so much better?" Denny asked as he admired his work.

While everyone was busy rehearsing the new lineup, the housekeepers were preparing the ladies' new rooms for them. They put the linens, blankets, and spreads on the beds and stocked their bathrooms with towels. Their rooms were ready for them at last.

The ladies couldn't wait to move in to their new rooms. They were running down the hallways, arms full of their possessions. They were all busy putting their things away and putting their personalized decorating touches around the rooms. Although the brothel supplied all the linens, blankets, and bedspreads, a lot of the ladies would buy their own comforters and throw pillows. They also brought stuffed animals, just to add their own personality to their rooms. They were like little kids, laughing and giggling and running into the other ladies' rooms to see how theirs were decorated. The housekeepers helped the ladies get settled in. Everyone was having a great time.

The ladies had beautiful new furniture, linens, pillows, blankets, and bedspreads. The ladies' rooms were all furnished and decorated identically. Those of you with children know you can't give something to one child and not to the other. I, at this point, had more than three hundred children! I have raised two boys and one girl. I have always said I would raise ten more boys before I would raise one more girl. It goes to show, you should be very careful what you wish for!

The ladies loved their rooms, and why wouldn't they? They were spacious, pristine, and inviting. The rooms were their homes during their stay at the brothel and now they felt like "home." Everything was so bright, cheery, and CLEAN.

I couldn't be outdone by my surroundings, so what would any madam do? Go shopping! Yes, a new wardrobe. I had quite an extensive wardrobe from my casino days. I can't tell you how many black-tie events I hosted for players, and I wouldn't be caught dead in the same outfit that I wore at a previous event. Would you? But that wardrobe was not befitting a madam, at least not this one. My wardrobe had to be kicked up a notch or two, from elaborate to flamboyant, from Princess Di to Queen Amidala.

I headed to the mall and bought a whole new wardrobe: sequins, glitter, sparkles, fur (faux fur, as I am an avid animal lover), evening gowns, long flowing jackets, hats, shoes of every color, and boots. The saleswomen who were helping me just kept bringing outfit after outfit.

"You must be going to a party, or a wedding, or taking a cruise," they would say.

"No, I'm buying new outfits for work," I'd answer.

"Where do you work?"

"I work at a brothel."

"Oh," they'd all say and look at one another with raised eyebrows.

Laughing to myself, I just kept shopping. Accessorizing was the icing on the cake for any outfit, so I donned necklaces, bracelets, and rings on practically every finger. Now that's a madam!

The commercial kitchen was under construction at the same time that the new brothel building was being built. The new kitchen would take a bit more time because so much equipment had been ordered, but hadn't arrived yet. Once it was completed, though, there would be no more "eat what I cook or go hungry." No more training table. The old trailer house kitchen, dining room, and living room would be gutted and turned into a dining facility for the ladies and staff. Individual tables and chairs would be placed throughout the new area, with a warm paint scheme, flowers on the tables, art on the walls. What an improvement it was going to be. Best of all, it would be clean, sparkling clean.

The outside was getting a makeover as well. The landscapers were working in the courtyard, planting palm trees and shrubs and laying sod. The pool and Jacuzzi were completed and it was beginning to look like a desert oasis. The three little trailers surrounded by dirt had disappeared. They now had a fresh coat of paint and were enveloped by a beautiful new building and lush greenery. The parking lot was paved and trees lined the entrances. I found that I no longer scrubbed my skin raw in the shower after my workday. Yes, the transition was taking place one step at a time.

Summer was once again upon us. But this summer would be different, at least for the ladies. No more lying out on a broken lounge chair surrounded by dirt with a spray bottle of water to cool off with. Now, they would lay out by the pool working on their tans — nude, of course. Couldn't have any tan lines. New pool furniture, chaises, chairs, tables; there was seating for forty around the pool, and the Jacuzzi would seat twelve comfortably. The ladies never complained about the summers in the desert anymore. They were loving life.

The VIP villas were still being built. We never seemed to have a problem getting construction crews to work at the brothel, especially in the summer. I remember one day a construction worker was nailing some plywood to the roof on one of the villas. He got up to get more nails or something, and was so enthralled looking at the ladies lying nude by the pool that he walked right off the roof. He broke his arm and his collarbone. You knew the guy had to be in pain, but the smile never left his face. Construction always seemed to take longer during the summer months; I can't imagine why!

With the villas nearing completion, the place was really shaping up. The villas were designed for the "high-rollers." At last, I would be dealing with people who wouldn't settle for anything less than the best of the best again. The transformation was something to behold. It was like going from the Bad News Bears to the New York Yankees, from the State Pen to Penn State. There was no comparison.

I decorated all the interiors of the buildings. The parlor had been expanded and received a complete makeover. Hardwood floors replaced that horrible shag carpet, artwork hung on the walls, armoires and settees were placed in the hallways. The place reeked of class.

The villas' floor plans were identical but each one was decorated differently. They were decorated ranging from the tie-dyed Woodstock era to European elegance. Each lady had outfits that complemented the décor of each villa so that their parties would become a complete experience for their guests. Gourmet meals and open bar service would be included with each villa party. This was the place to make fantasies become realities. You could be anyone you wanted to be here.

What a place! The dark, dingy hallways — gone. Blood-red shag carpet – gone. Those horrid wall sconces — gone. Worn and tattered furniture – gone. Old linens and towels with who knows how much DNA on them – gone. The filthy, tiny, cramped rooms for the ladies — gone. The chandelier, however, was still hanging in its original place, but the crystals now sparkled and danced with life.

Naturally, with a bigger facility to take care of, more staff would be needed. I was quite the opposite of Donald Trump. I was hiring everybody — cooks, security, shift managers, bartenders, and housekeepers. This was a resort, people. It really was.

Housekeeping was an integral part of the operation. If the brothel didn't look clean, what would people think of the ladies? Even a rumor of a disease could put a brothel out of business in a heartbeat. Cleanliness was a must. It was one area in which I would not settle for anything less than perfection. It determined our mere existence. The new housekeepers did a terrific job. The place just shined. Time after time, customers would comment on the cleanliness of the property. "You must have a helluva housekeeping department, because this place is immaculate!" they would say.

I did. I couldn't count how many people were amazed when they walked through those parlor doors. No one expected to see what they saw.

It was such an exhilarating feeling to exceed someone's expectations.

I hired our new maintenance man from the crew that built the new brothel. He was a Spanish man who spoke broken English and knew the place inside and out. I was lucky to get Fernando. The ladies loved him, too. In addition to fixing whatever broke on the property, Fernando fixed the ladies' shoes, purses, cars. It didn't matter what it was, if it was broken, Fernando could fix it. Fernando was definitely a refreshing change from the maintenance man who was working there when I started.

But as good as Fernando was at fixing things, it always bothered me that the tanning bed would break every spring and Fernando couldn't figure out what was wrong with it until the fall. That was, until one summer day. Fernando was working on the pool pump while we were getting ready for our big annual shindig. My husband and a friend of ours, James, were helping me get ready for the festivities. Taking a break from the sweltering heat, Fernando, James, and my husband grabbed a spot of shade and were admiring the scenery, which happened to be some ladies who were sunbathing. My husband asked Fernando, "Is it like this every day?"

"Why you think I don't fix the tanning bed?" Fernando replied.

Classic.

With the new facility, the clientele seemed to upgrade themselves as well. The ladies were all of "runway" caliber now. I remember when they used to be "run away" caliber: You'd take one look at them and you'd want to run away. Now they were gorgeous. The beauty of the property could not hold a candle to the beauty of the ladies. The days of foul-mouthed, comic book tattooed, rude, crude, and tough ladies were gone. Now, don't get me wrong, we still had a few bumps in the road as far as the ladies were concerned, and trust me, we'll get to that. But overall, WOW!

Along with this fancy place came the big bucks. You just knew the minute you walked in that this was going to cost you. Appearances are so important. They set the tone for what a customer may come to expect. Image is everything! This place made a statement: "There's no way you're getting off cheap here, pal, just look around you." That was our statement. It was like the gaming business all over again. I was surrounded by beauty: beautiful property, beautiful rooms, beautiful furnishings, beautiful gardens, and most importantly, beautiful ladies.

We almost had it all: a gorgeous brothel, stunning ladies, and guys with money. The brothel had gone through an amazing transition. The transition was a little slower, however, from a customer service standpoint. I had to take the employees from their "Would you like fries with that?" mentality to "And for your dining pleasure we offer . . ." mentality. They had to make the transition from "wretched" to "resort." Easier said than done.

I did, however, have a big advantage. With so many years in the casino industry, I can't begin to tell you how many millions of dollars of customer service training I have had. You see, casinos typically will spend ten times their marketing budgets on customer service training. The gaming gurus have mastered the art of customer service. In the gaming industry you can see four or five of your competitors from your own doorstep. They know far too well that they all offer roughly the same games, same odds, same comps, etc., and therefore they focus on their people. Their employees and the customer service they extend is what will make one casino different from another.

During the entire construction process, I worked closely with the staff on customer service. The construction went a lot smoother than the customer service training did. There were no resorts in Pahrump. There wasn't even any place to go where you would get dressed up. I will admit, at times, I had to work very hard to contain my urge to choke some of them. That was certainly not something I learned in my vast training in customer service, but it was a product of human nature at its breaking point. In thinking about it, I have to say in my defense that I didn't choke anyone and that may be attributed to my vast customer service training, coupled with the fact that I had no desire to go to prison. There has to be another way to get through to them.

I got it! New wardrobes! That would speed things up. When you look good, you feel good. When you feel good, you have a better attitude. When you have a better attitude, you are more receptive to change. It's a chain reaction. Perfect!

The bartenders would wear black slacks and tuxedo shirts. Housekeepers would wear crisp, white smocks. The kitchen staff would sport chef's garb. Shift managers would dress to the nines. Security would have logoed brothel shirts. Also, I would order name tags with our logo on it for everyone, their name and position right next to the logo. Recognition — everybody loves recognition. This was going to be great. And it was. Everyone felt good about themselves and their jobs. They took pride in their positions. They were finally catching on to the customer service training.

You have to keep in mind that before, if you went to the bar and ordered a Cosmopolitan, the bartender would have handed you a magazine.

Things were looking up. The brothel had a whole new air about it. There wasn't another brothel like it anywhere. Customer service wasn't even a consideration at any other brothel. At this one, we set the standard. The bar had been raised high.

You know, I thought, this place ain't so bad after all.

Construction was finally completed and the day had arrived when we were going to debut the villas. Not five minutes passed before one of the ladies came to the counter to book her first VIP villa party. The shift manager looked like a deer in headlights. She was so perplexed, she just froze. I'm not sure if she was overwhelmed by booking the villa or if it was the amount of money that was being spent. Both were new territory.

"Calm down and just take it one step at a time," I reassured her. First things first. Take the money. Now, call security to open the villa. Next, take their food order. Food! Oh, shit, the cook went home already. No worries. I'm sure we can throw together a deli plate, cheese platter, something. My husband was there working on the cameras; he could conjure up something, I'm sure.

The new kitchen wasn't completed yet. We were still waiting for the equipment. Can you believe it? My husband was flying around the old kitchen trying to find two plates that matched, as the new china hadn't been delivered yet either. What a mess.

"Just cover the entire plate with meats and the other one with cheeses and then they'll match," I said.

"Well, what happens when they eat the food and then notice the plates don't match?"

"Let's hope the guy has more interest in the lady than he does in the plates," I said.

A little bit of fresh parsley, olives, gherkins, fancy toothpicks, okay, not too bad.

The food was delivered to the villa, along with a bottle of champagne. A little hectic, but I don't think the customer noticed a thing. Just then the shift manager's phone rang. It was the villa calling.

"We wanted to put some porn movies on, but there's no VCR."

Another job for my husband. "We'll get one right out to you."

My husband wasn't exactly thrilled when I told him he needed to hook up a VCR in the villa. He had argued with Sam when the villas were being built that VCRs should be put in all the villas. Sam was adamant that they didn't need them. So much for Sam's theory.

My husband and his buddy, James, are geniuses when it comes to cameras, recording equipment, basically anything with a wire. They put in all the cameras and security equipment. They built a TV station so the ladies didn't all have to watch the same thing at the same time.

They ran all the conduit, cabling, everything that was low voltage. After it was all said and done, there were forty security cameras throughout the property, all in public areas. None were in the ladies' rooms or the villas or any other rooms used for partying.

My husband pulled a VCR from the security office and rushed out to the villa. He knocked on the door. "This will just take me a minute and you'll be all set," he said.

He quickly hooked up the VCR while his captive audience was lying on the couch, naked, enjoying his the plate and watching him intently. Walking toward the door, he said, "Sorry for the intrusion."

"Not a problem. Would you like to stay?" the lady asked.

"We don't mind if you watch," the customer added.

"No, that's okay, I'm good," he said and walked out. Another problem solved.

They were all set now, so we could all relax, right? Wrong! Not an hour went by and the phone rang again. It was the villa calling. "We wanted to take a bubble bath, but there is no hot water."

"I'll send someone right out."

You guessed it: my husband again.

"Did they turn on the hot water heaters when they turned the villas over to you?" he asked.

"I don't know. They gave me the keys, that's all I know."

Again, he ran out to the villa. "Sorry, this will take just one more minute." Nope, they hadn't turned them on. "Just give it about thirty minutes and you should be good to go."

"Thank you. Are you sure you won't join us?"

"No, thanks. I'm still good."

As time progressed, villa parties would become more routine. They quickly became the most sought-after feature of the brothel, other than the ladies, of course. The amounts of money spent for the villas never ceased to amaze me.

The attention to detail in the villas was second to none. Everything within the walls of each villa was tied to its respective theme. Not the slightest detail was overlooked. The villas were very private, elegant and intimate. This, coupled with the lineups constantly improving, contributed to the villas being the most profitable outlet of the entire brothel. Forty thousand, fifty thousand, even ninety thousand dollars just for one night, one lady and one villa. Incredible!

The new kitchen finally was completed. The equipment was delivered and installed. New china, glassware, silverware, linen napkins, crystal salt and pepper shakers — everything was new. A special food menu was put together just for the villas. Private villa, open bar, gourmet meal, seductive woman . . . could it get any better than that?

Chapter Five

LADIES AND GENTLEMEN

I remember one night a helicopter landed in the courtyard of the brothel. Out of the helicopter stepped a man in his mid-forties, hair graying around his temples, about five feet ten inches tall, and a little vertically challenged for his weight. He swaggered as he walked. I met him in the parlor.

"Welcome," I greeted him.

"Are you the madam?"

"I am."

"Well, madam, I came to check out your wares."

I seated him on the couch and called for a lineup. The lineup was exquisite, and I could see that even "Mr. High and Mighty" was impressed. He picked Missy, a beautiful blonde with long, flowing hair that fell softly just below her waist. Missy stood almost six feet, but that was in her seven-inch heels. She proudly displayed 48DDD natural breasts bursting out of her black lace bra. She was truly a vision. Missy escorted Mr. High and Mighty to her room. Let the games begin!

The negotiation lasted only about three minutes. Mr. High and Mighty was so taken with Missy's beauty that he anxiously agreed to whatever she said.

"A villa it is then," Missy said in her sweet, sultry voice with just a hint of a Southern drawl. "You relax and I'll be right back."

Missy scurried to the office with her fists full of cash. Her eyes were as big as her breasts as the shift manager counted hundred after hundred after hundred.

"Can you believe it? Eighty thousand dollars! I am really a high-class hooker, aren't I, Mom?"

"You're right about one thing, sweetheart," I replied. "You are certainly high class but you're no hooker. How many hookers do you know that make eighty thousand dollars for one party? Honey, there's a big difference between a hooker and a lady, and you, my dear, are one helluva lady. Good job."

The shift manager called for security to unlock the villa and Missy went to get her gentleman. I was passing through the parlor as they were on their way out to the villa.

"Madam, do you have fine wines here?"

"Of course," I replied.

"Well, I am sort of a wine connoisseur and I would like a bottle of your finest red wine, if you wouldn't mind."

"Not at all. Since you are a connoisseur of sorts, I'll tell you what I'll do. I will pull my best bottle from my private reserve, just for you and your beautiful lady."

"The madam's private reserve, I like the sound of that," said Mr. High and Mighty.

"Consider it done. I'll have it sent right out to you."

With that, off they went.

We serve wine in our bar, of course. What bar doesn't serve wine? But fine wine? You've got to be kidding me. Okay, think. Got it! I went to one of the china closets in the parlor. At that point, I was so grateful that I had purchased two Waterford decanters for the china closet. I took out one of the decanters and headed to the bar. Behind the bar, I started grabbing some red wine splits, unscrewed the caps and started pouring them in the decanter. That's right, you read it correctly, unscrewed the caps. I called security over my radio and had him meet me in the bar. I polished two wine glasses, found a silver tray and there it was . . . fine wine. Security delivered the wine to the villa.

About an hour later there was a call. "Madam, the gentleman from the villa would like to speak with you. I'll transfer him back." Here we go. He couldn't possibly really be a connoisseur, could he?

"Madam, I'm calling about the wine."

"Yes, how can I help you?"

"You wouldn't happen to have another bottle hidden somewhere, would you? I must say, that was the best red I've ever had."

"You know, I just might. Let me check and, if so, I'll send it right out." I knew he wasn't a connoisseur!

I grabbed the other Waterford decanter and headed back to the bar. Did you ever have déjà vu? I called again for security. This time, the instructions were a little different. "Deliver this wine to the villa. When you deliver it, you MUST bring the empty decanter back. This is very important. Do not come back without that empty decanter." God forbid Mr. High and Mighty wanted another bottle of fine wine!

Well, he enjoyed himself so much, not to mention the fine wine, that he extended his party for another forty thousand dollars.

We never did carry fine wine. I really didn't see the need for it as long as we had Waterford decanters!

Each villa party went smoother than the last. I couldn't believe this was the same place. The only hint of the dirty little trailers were the trailers themselves. But they weren't dirty anymore. They had been gutted and remodeled. The trailers became the area we referred to as "the back of the house." The trailers now housed amenities just for the ladies: lounge, salon, massage room, computers, dining facility. The place was not only a resort for the customers, but for the ladies as well.

The back of the house was where most of the ladies spent their time when they weren't working. It was also where most of the conflicts among the ladies took place. Having raised a daughter, I am a firm believer that there is a genetic flaw in the female gender. You see, girls truly believe that if they're not talking, they're not breathing. Girls are also under the impression that everyone is entitled to her opinion.

Snide remarks became routine, especially when someone had booked a large party, which was a daily occurrence, I was happy to say. And because they are girls, can they just let it go? Absolutely not! Before you knew it, World War III had broken out because now the spectators have become participants as well. No one can keep her mouth shut! I could hear them through the hallways and all the way in my office.

Here I go, running down the hallway to the back of the house.

"What the hell is going on?" Now I have fifteen of them talking at once, each telling me her side of the story. Of course, fifteen ladies, fifteen different stories.

You know, I was always disappointed that with all the running I used to do around that property, I thought I should be thinner. Hmmm. Maybe it was my metabolism. Oh well, back to the case at hand.

"Quiet! Everybody be quiet." Silence. Once the "mother voice" kicked in, they all stopped dead in their tracks. "Now, one at a time, what happened?"

I listened to them, one after the other. "She said . . . and then she said . . . and then she rolled her eyes," and so on. At that moment it dawned on me: I finished raising my own kids and now I was raising someone else's. Great.

The ladies all referred to me as "Mom." I received more Mother's Day cards in the years I worked in the brothel than over all the years that

I raised my own children. These ladies were my children, regardless of how old they were. For many of them, I was the only stable figure in their lives. And they didn't have to be at the brothel to call me for help. They would call me even if they weren't at the brothel. I remember getting phone calls in the middle of the night from them because they had a fight with their boyfriend, or because their child ran away, or they lost their dog, crashed their car, they were sick . . . you name it. I never minded their calls and always talked with them until they calmed down and weren't crying anymore. (Those phone calls prompted the phone to be moved back to my side of the bed. When I worked in the casino, the phone was moved to my side because of all the late-night calls. After I left gaming, it had moved to my husband's side.)

Laughter is a universal remedy for most problems, so I would tell the ladies stories that would make them laugh. All the calls ended the same way: "I love you, Mom." And I loved them . . . still do.

I remember when I was on a cruise. I finally got away for a week and, boy, did I need it. At last, cell phones worked sporadically, very sporadically. Fresh air, beaches, cocktails . . . this was the life! It was about midnight when my cell phone rang. Who the hell could that be? I answered the phone and heard, "Why can't I get room five? Why is she in it? Mom, I want room five."

Are you kidding me?

"Chris, settle down."

"Mom, I want room five. Jen is in it. Kick her out and give it to me."

"Chris, did Jen arrive at the brothel before you?"

"Yes, but that doesn't matter, I want room five."

The ladies were booked into the rooms based on when they arrived at the brothel. First come, first served. Simple, right? Wrong! Chris and Jen had, shall we say, a personality conflict. They slightly resembled one another, and so they thought each other's respective customers should have been theirs. Both were average height, petite and brunette, although one had short hair and the other long. And, oh yes, they were both girls! I knew if anyone else were in room five other than Jen, Chris never would have called.

I said to Chris, "Next time, arrive earlier and perhaps you won't have this problem."

Naturally, this wasn't what Chris wanted to hear, so she kept whining, "But Mom, that isn't fair."

"Chris, what do you expect me to do? I'm in the middle of the ocean. What room are you in, Chris?"

"Room six."

"Oh, don't even go there. You called me in the middle of the night, in the middle of the ocean, and you're right next door? Are you insane? Go to bed."

"All right. Good night, Mom."

My husband asked, "Who was that?" Did he even have to ask? They were just like kids. At times you want to kill them, but most of the time they made you smile.

The ladies could be extremely thoughtful at times. They earned a good living and they spoiled themselves — that is, if they didn't have a pimp. Those who didn't have a pimp would travel a lot when they were not working. They might bring back a souvenir from their travels and couldn't wait to give it to me. They would be so excited and tell me all about their adventures. Their eyes would light up as they talked about what they did and what they saw. "Mom, you should have been there. You should have seen it. You would have loved it." I remember sitting in my office listening to their stories and smiling. Life is all about making memories. Memories are all we will have to take with us when we leave. Knowing the ladies as well as I did, I took comfort in knowing they were making some good memories and hoped those good memories would replace some of their bad memories. They were so happy and I was so happy for them.

Quite a few of the ladies were married and had children. They would ask for advice when their children wouldn't behave as they thought they should, not realizing that they themselves sometimes would act in the same way as they were describing their children's behavior. As I would listen, I couldn't help but think about how hard it must be for them not to have their "real mom" there to help them. It doesn't matter how old you are, there are times when only your mom can give you the shoulder that you need. But to the ladies, I was their "real mom," and so I listened, I counseled, I yelled when I had to, and I held them when they needed that, too. Regardless of their age, sometimes a hug and a kiss still made everything seem better.

There was one lady, Houston, who had a dependency on recreational stimulants, and Houston had an extremely hard time with the zero-tolerance drug policy. So, in order to compensate for not doing drugs while she was working, Houston would load up on whatever it was she took before she got to work. She was a very pretty lady and always showed up at the brothel looking like hell. She probably hadn't slept for days, trying to satisfy her hunger for the recreational stimulants that she would be missing over the next two weeks. Normally, Houston would arrive at the brothel, see the doctor, and then pass out until the next day when she cleared her medical exams and was able to work. By the next day, you couldn't believe it was the same lady. What a transformation! You would have never guessed that she was high and out of her mind just twenty-four hours before.

That was, until her last trip to the brothel. Houston arrived, as usual, in her own world. She saw the doctor and then went to her room. It was about nine o'clock in the evening when she started screaming bloody murder. I ran to her room (more running!) and there she was, crying and screaming and covered in blood. Houston had slit her wrists. She didn't even know that she had done it. I called over the radio for security to bring towels, water, and ice. I called the paramedics and they rushed her to the hospital. Blood-soaked myself, I remember being up all night long, worrying, waiting to hear something, anything. My phone rings all the time, why isn't it ringing now? Can't someone pick up the damn phone and call me? Finally, it rang.

"Thank God." I hung up the phone. She was going to be all right. She would be transported to the psychiatric ward for a mandatory three days of observation. Houston called me after she was released. "Mom, I'm so sorry. I don't know how this happened," she said. She was sobbing so hard that she couldn't catch her breath.

"Everything is going to be all right, sweetheart. Everything will be fine. I want you to check yourself into rehab. Can you do that for me?" She did. Houston still keeps in touch with me. She has been clean and sober for five years now, and the calls still end the same. "I love you, Mom."

Physical altercations were not permitted at the brothel whatsoever. If two ladies became involved in a fight, both were removed from the brothel, never to return. I was working in my office one afternoon, minding my own business, when one of the ladies came running in. "Mom, Mom, hurry up. I think she's going to hit her." I ran to the dining room. (You see what I mean? I should be thinner!)

There they were, two ladies, in each other's face, screaming. I got between them and separated them. It was Cynthia and Jewels. Cynthia had worked at the brothel for quite some time and I'd never had a problem with her before. Jewels was a brand new lady.

I asked Cynthia what happened. "I was just coming in to get some lunch and this girl, who I don't even know, just says, 'Fuck you, bitch.' I went up to her and said, 'Are you talking to me?' She says, 'Yeah. bitch, I'm talking to you.'"

I asked Jewels if that was true. Jewels said, "Yeah, fuck that bitch." At that point I informed Jewels that we don't tolerate that type of behavior at this brothel and that she would have to pack her things and leave. Jewels said, "That bitch fucked my boyfriend." Apparently, her boyfriend was a customer of Cynthia's, unbeknownst to Cynthia. I again told Jewels that she needed to pack and leave. Jewels started screaming, "You can't make me leave. No one can make me leave." That's when I enlightened Jewels that she was wrong. "You're leaving, one way or another. You can either leave of your own accord or you can leave by me physically throwing you out. It doesn't make a difference to me, but rest assured, either way you're leaving."

Just as I was finishing my sentence, Jewels wound up, from the basement, and threw a round-house punch. I caught her fist in mid-air and enlighten her once again, "The smart money goes on the old, fat broad."

I radioed for housekeeping to pack up Jewels' things and had security escort her off property. Well, there's nothing like a little excitement for a mid-afternoon pick-me-up, although, at my age, a cup of espresso would have been sufficient!

Then there was Charlotte. She was another new lady, first trip to the brothel. The ladies came from all over the world. They came from as far away as Australia, Russia, Egypt, the Dominican Republic, Brazil, Thailand, Vietnam, all over. They would e-mail their photos, and based on their looks and age, of course (they had to be at least twenty-one to work at the brothel), I would book them to work at the brothel. All ladies were booked based on availability. This brothel became so popular that a lot of the ladies would book their schedules up to a year in advance to ensure we had room for them. You couldn't expect a lady to travel halfway around the world for an interview. So, I booked them based on their looks and hoped that their personalities were just as attractive. For the most part they were. But not in Charlotte's case.

Charlotte was at the brothel for about two days before we learned that she was nuts. At four in the morning I received a call from the shift manager. "Charlotte is screaming in her room. I have a lady partying in the room next door. The customer is complaining and she has awakened all the other ladies. I sent security down there but she won't stop screaming."

"Tell her if she doesn't stop screaming that she is going to have to leave."

The madam was the only one who had the authority to throw a lady off the property. Twenty minutes later the phone rang again. "She stopped for about ten minutes, but she's screaming again."

"What is she screaming about?"

"I don't know, she just keeps screaming about how God is coming for her."

I instructed the shift manager to throw her out. I wasn't going to have an unhappy customer and let this lunatic disrupt his party, not to mention the entire house. Okay, back to sleep. Ten minutes later, you got it, the phone rang again. "She won't leave."

"I'll be right there."

I got up, got dressed, and headed to the brothel. After making so many trips from Las Vegas in the middle of the night to "put out fires" at the brothel, I had decided to sell the house in Las Vegas and move to Pahrump. So, luckily, I was only ten minutes away instead of an hour. I arrived at the brothel, walked into the office and the shift manager was on the phone. It was an inside line. "Is that Charlotte?" The shift manager nodded her head yes. I took the phone and informed Charlotte that she had to leave the brothel. She hung up on me. "Bitch." I ran down to her room, and as luck would have it, she was in one of the rooms farthest down the long hallway. (Are you getting this whole "thinner" thing that I'm battling with?)

Security was right behind me. "Do you want me to go in with you?" the security officer asked.

"No, just stand by."

I went in and there was Charlotte, sitting on the bed, yelling at God. I told her she needed to start packing. She informed me she wasn't leaving.

"On the contrary, you are. You can pack or I will pack for you."

"Don't touch my shit," Charlotte said.

"Then start packing." She didn't, so I did. I got her luggage from the closet and started putting her things in it. She sprang off the bed and lunged across the room toward me. I grabbed her as she frantically swinging her fists. She wasn't swinging very hard, but she was swinging very fast. I caught one fist, then the other, then the other again. That went on for about ten swings and I was starting to get tired. I'm old, I'm fat, I'm tired, it's almost five o'clock in the morning . . . give me a break! I pinned her up against the wall and held her there by her throat. Finally, she settled down. That may have been the result of a lack of oxygen. Surprisingly, she was now convinced that she was in fact leaving. I called for security, who was standing by outside the door, and he came in.

"Is everything okay? I heard a lot of banging going on in here."

"Everything is fine. Can you please show Ms. Charlotte to the door? Thanks."

I had no idea that this job was going to be so physical. I'm not in any shape for this kind of thing. Who would have thought that you would have to be physically fit to be a madam? This job is going to kill me!

All of the other ladies were clamoring in the hallway. "The excitement is over, ladies. You can all go back to bed now. Good night, ladies." I waited until I knew all the ladies were settled in their beds, said good night to the shift manager, lit a cigarette, and went back home. Naturally, I couldn't fall back asleep. The sun was starting to come up. Oh, what the hell, coffee sounds good.

An hour later, my husband came into the kitchen, "Couldn't sleep?" he asked.

"No, it's such a beautiful day I thought I would just get up early and enjoy it." He had not heard the phone ring. He never knew I was gone.

Those beautiful ladies: so different; so childlike; so many! They have given me so many memories, and for that, I thank them.

I didn't smoke when I started working at the brothel. I used to, but I had quit about eight years before. It didn't take long before cigarettes were part of my daily regimen. It was the only legal thing I could think of to preserve my sanity. I'd run into old friends and they'd say, "I thought you quit."

"I did."

"You're smoking."

"I am."

"How come?"

"I work in a brothel with twenty-five ladies who are all PMSing at the same time. What would you do?"

"I'd smoke."

Chapter Six

A 24/7 Business

It's true. ~~When ladies live in close proximity, as~~ they do in the brothel, their monthly cycles often coincide. Can you imagine twenty-five ladies all going through their time of the month at the same time? I don't condone the use of drugs and have never used them myself, but I now have a better understanding of their appeal!

The ladies work even when they are having their monthly cycle. The brothel business doesn't stop, no matter what. There's a trick of the trade: black condoms. They use black condoms during their monthly cycle.

Condoms are used for all activities, including oral techniques. It's mandatory; it's the law. If a customer wants to perform orally on a lady, there's also a condom for that. A "dental dam" is a female condom. It is made out of the same latex that male condoms are made of. It is a flat latex condom that is placed over the female genital area and conforms to the shape of the female genitalia. There is "zero exchange" of any bodily fluids. That includes kissing. Absolutely "zero exchange" of any bodily fluids.

Regardless of the circumstances, the brothel business never stops. One night we lost power at the brothel. That actually happened on numerous occasions. Being in the middle of nowhere, we weren't at the top of the list as far as the power company was concerned, so our power was restored, it seemed, after the company was through with everyone else's problems.

Anyway, there we were in total darkness. We placed some battery-operated lanterns in the bar. The customers stayed and even more came in. One gentleman asked if he could have a lineup. "Of course you can."

I rounded up the ladies, which took a little bit of time as the PA system and the red lights weren't functioning.

"How can we have a lineup, Mom? You can't even see your hand in front of your face."

"Don't worry, I have a plan."

I called, "Ladies from the right; ladies from the left," and when the ladies were all lined up, I handed a lantern to the lady who was farthest to the right. "Make sure you hold the lantern up to your face so the customer can see you and pass it to the next lady after you introduce yourself." And that's what they did. It actually was a very sexy lineup as you could see the silhouette of the lady's body as she held the lantern up to her face. The customer loved it.

As I recall, we did a lot of lineups during power outages. It was different, and after all, wasn't that why most people were there in the first place? Customers of the brothel were those who were looking for something different, something exciting, something new. It didn't necessarily mean that married customers were unhappy in their marriages. Just as the ladies had their reasons for working at a brothel, customers had their reasons for visiting one.

The single guys who came to the brothel were easy to figure out. They wanted sexual experiences, but they wanted "safe sex" without a relationship. Married guys had a variety of different reasons. Some would come to the brothel because their wives had taken ill, perhaps seriously ill, and although they loved their wives and were there to take care of them, their sexual needs couldn't be met within the marriage. There were others whose wives encouraged them to visit the brothel. Some wives even paid for their husband's parties. I have spoken to many wives who wanted to buy their husband a party for his birthday, anniversary or just to do something "special" for him. Some would be on business trips in Las Vegas and everyone knows "What Happens in Vegas, Stays in Vegas." Even more so at the brothel.

As years went by, I realized that the parallels between gaming and prostitution were numerous. Actually, the brothel was just like a casino. It was a 24/7 operation, just like a casino. The brothel offered complimentary limousine service to customers, just like a casino. The brothel catered to its customers' each and every desire, just like a casino. Customer service at the brothel was at the excellence level, just like a casino. And the brothel made its money the same way casinos make theirs: time on device.

The longer you stay in a casino, the better chance the casino has of getting your money. That's why casinos accommodate their customers the way they do. The brothel did the same. We catered to our customers, just like a casino. The only difference was, the brothel took all the gamble out of it — you knew you would get lucky there!

It didn't take long before the word got out . . . this was the place to be. Word of mouth was the second-best advertising vehicle; the Internet was first. Brothels, at the time, were not allowed to advertise. No printed collateral, no magazine ads, no newspaper ads, no TV commercials, no radio spots. So we had a multimillion-dollar adult resort and we couldn't tell anybody about it. I give a lot of credit to Shawn. He spent a lot of money on something he knew he couldn't launch with any type of marketing campaign. Pretty gutsy.

It just goes to show: Sex sells! The numbers kept growing and growing.

Shawn used to get the numbers via e-mail every day and he called me many times, asking, "Am I reading these figures right?"

"Yes, sir, you are."

It was unbelievable. Thinking back, it was a little unsettling. I bet I gave away millions over the years. What a schmuck! I wonder if I could go back and amend my taxes. You think I could write that off as a donation?

But just like any other business, the more money, the more problems. The ladies were becoming more and more competitive. Every lady wanted every potential dollar. Naturally, that couldn't happen, so "dirty hustling" became a viable edge. Dirty hustling is defined as a lady calling undue attention to herself (by any means possible).

There were rules, and as time progressed, so did the rules. When a lady was speaking with a gentleman at the bar, it was prohibited for another lady to approach them. Keep in mind that these ladies were creative — very creative. So, knowing they couldn't approach, they might walk by a lady sitting with a gentleman and "accidentally" bump into the gentleman's chair. "Oh, excuse me. Are you all right, sweetheart? I'm so sorry."

That's all it took and all hell would break loose. The ladies would be in my office in a split second.

"She's dirty hustling."

"I accidentally bumped into the guy's chair. All I said was I'm sorry."

It didn't take long for the situation to deteriorate. It was the whole "girl" thing again. Girls can go from zero to bitch in about 2.3 seconds!

The ladies were not allowed to make eye contact with a gentleman who was sitting with another lady. They couldn't wave, smile, say hello; they had to just leave them be.

But you show me one girl who can let anything be. Of course, when I spoke to them about it, nine out of ten times their reasoning was, "I had one too many drinks. You know me, Mom. I would never do anything like that. I'm sorry." You bet I knew them and the alcohol had nothing to do with it. Thus, the "No Drink List" was born. When a lady couldn't control her behavior because of alcohol, she was placed on the "No Drink List." Needless to say, alcohol was no longer an excuse they chose to use.

Ladies were also placed on the "No Drink List" if they checked into the brothel with medication that indicated it was "not to be taken with alcohol" or "alcohol may intensify effects" or anything of that nature. Oh, they checked in with tons of medication. We had a "zero drug tolerance" program in effect, remember? So, they brought Lortabs, Vicodin, and who knows what other legal prescriptions. They had more pills than any pharmacy.

We secured their medications at the shift manager's desk when they checked in. The shift manager would dispense their medication to them just as prescribed on the label. There was no way I was going to let them keep their meds in their rooms. When they wouldn't be taking more than the prescribed doses, they would be selling pills to the other ladies. You had to be one step ahead of them all the time. Chess — I never liked chess. Okay, it's your move, ladies!

The ladies weren't permitted to approach a customer in the bar before the customer had his drink. You would think that would be pretty easy to comply with. It doesn't take a Philadelphia lawyer to figure out if a guy has had a drink or not, right? But things weren't as simple as they appeared, I guess. "Mom, I didn't think he was drinking." He came to the bar, of course he's drinking! "Mom, I know this guy." Doesn't matter — wait until he has his drink. "Sorry, Mom, I forgot." Forgot? How hard was this? It went on and on.

Dirty hustling could take place in the lineup, too. The ladies were supposed to stand still in the lineup until it was their turn to walk up and introduce themselves. When they introduced themselves, all they were permitted to say was, "Hi, my name is . . ." That's it. Easy, right? Well, it would be if they weren't girls! They wiggle, they giggle — they dirty hustle. All it took was one girl one time and the whole house was in an uproar. Girls! I'm telling you . . . it's a genetic flaw!

The bar was always a source of excitement. The brothel didn't allow pimps or significant others of the ladies on the property. One morning there were a couple of guys in the bar and a couple of the ladies went out to talk with them. All of a sudden the shit hit the fan. I ran out of my office and got between the two guys. I instructed the ladies to go to their rooms. The two guys happened to be pimps. Apparently one of the ladies who had just left the bar used to work for one of the pimps, left him, and went to work for the other pimp. Women who leave one pimp for another are called "Choosy Suzies." Choosy Suzies are not very well liked by the other women who have pimps. That was what the argument was about. Dismissing the ladies didn't end the argument. These guys wanted to kill each other. Normally, I wouldn't have been opposed to the idea, but not here; not at my brothel. The situation was escalating quickly and they laughed at me when I told them they had to leave. They weren't laughing when I grabbed an autographed bat off the wall and started swinging it at them like a lunatic! They both ran out the door yelling "That bitch is crazy!" and never came back. At that moment I was very grateful that the bar had a sports theme. That memorabilia had really come in handy. Laugh at me, indeed! Who in their right mind would get between two pimps? Hmmm, they may have had a point.

That was just another day at the brothel. If you're looking for something different than your typical nine-to-five, job, I'd recommend becoming a madam.

Chapter Seven

MEET THE LADIES

There were so many ladies at the brothel over the years, it's hard to know where to begin. Each was unique in many ways, yet similar in so many others. Well, let's take it from the top.

Alice

I remember when Alice first came to the brothel. She was tough. Beautiful, but tough. She didn't speak with anyone, not the other ladies or the staff. Conversation was kept to a minimum, by Alice's choice. She had a hardened look and a glare that could cut right through you — so much so that the other ladies were afraid to look her in the eye. She commanded respect just by her demeanor. She walked with confidence, not arrogance, just confidence. The other ladies would give Alice a wide berth when passing by her in the hallways or the bar. It was clear to see that Alice intimidated the other ladies and the staff. I suppose it was her silence, coupled with her confidence, that made her appear unapproachable.

Alice, nor any other lady, ever intimidated me. I think that can be attributed to growing up on the East Coast. Where I grew up, you had to be tough to survive. Back then, areas were still segregated by nationality. There was the Italian section, Jewish section, Irish section, black section, etc. For the most part, people stayed in their own sections, but every now and then they would wander beyond and on to your turf. That didn't sit well with most, and no one I knew had a problem letting anyone know that this would not be tolerated.

Alice was an East Coast girl as well. When she arrived at the brothel and came to the shift manager's desk to check in to her room, I looked at her and knew that under that hard shell was a sweet and caring person. She caught me looking at her out of the corner of her eye. She snapped her head around and there was that glare. You know the one: "If looks could kill . . ." I just smiled at her and said, "Welcome." With a smirk on her face, she turned back to the shift manager, never uttering a word.

As time progressed, Alice remained silent. She spoke to no one, other than the customers, of course. She worked the bar magically. Alice had a beautiful smile, the kind that would light up her entire face. Blond hair, brown eyes, big chest, beautiful legs, and toned body. She wasn't very tall, maybe five feet four, but remember, you have to add at least six inches to every lady's height to allow for her high heels. (I wouldn't walk on anything that high without a net!) Alice was in her mid-thirties.

I would listen to her negotiations. There was no doubt about it, Alice was a pro. She was very well spoken and a quick wit, which surprised anyone who monitored her negotiations. And what a sweet voice! She really should speak more often, I thought.

It didn't take Alice long to adjust to this house. She had worked at brothels up north, in the Reno area, before she came to us. She was a professional, something else that would intimidate some of the other ladies. Alice had been in the business for about nine years before she came to our brothel. She had quite a following. Her customers would follow her no matter where she worked.

I remember when she booked her first party. It was for nine thousand dollars. She wasn't in her room thirty minutes when I saw her seat her customer on the couch to be shown out. I walked up to her customer and asked him if he had enjoyed his visit. "This was the most memorable experience I've ever had," he said with a smile that stretched from ear to ear. "She's incredible. I think I'm in love!" I showed him to the door and told him that I hoped to see him again soon. "No worries," he said, still smiling. "I'll be here every time Alice is here." And he was.

It didn't take long before we became accustomed to Alice's parties. If you wanted to spend the entire night with Alice, six figures would be customary. In all the years Alice worked at the brothel I never received one complaint from any of her customers. Alice extended customer service at the excellence level, the sign of a true professional.

As time passed, Alice became more sociable. The first time she passed me in the hallway and said "Hello," I almost fell over. I remember looking back over my shoulder to see if someone was behind me. She couldn't be talking to me, could she? But she was. She started speaking to the staff and we all learned that she had a wonderful personality. I would come to learn that Alice supported her mother, her sister, and her grandmother, all of whom resided on the East Coast. She was married and was the sole supporter of the family. She invested her money in real estate and had many holdings in California and Nevada. She was smart, even though she had only an eighth-grade education.

Alice ran away from an abusive home when she was twelve years old and had worked the streets to survive. She met a man, who would later become her husband, and then entered the world of legal prostitution. It took many years to come to know Alice the way I did. I remember the first time she called me "Mom." It took a while but as Alice grew comfortable in her environment, she would let her guard down just a bit.

To this day, though, Alice will never put herself in a position where she may be vulnerable. To this day, she still commands respect, not to mention lots of money.

Brenda

What a sweetheart. The minute you saw her, you were drawn to her. Long, straight blond hair, beautiful blue eyes, tall, slender, and big boobs. (Really, who ever saw a flat-chested prostitute?) Brenda was one of the most kind, compassionate, and sincere women you would ever meet. Everyone looked forward to Brenda booking in to the brothel. She would chat and share stories and I can't remember anyone who didn't like Brenda. She was truly a joy to have in the house.

Her customers loved her, too. She would have appointments booked regularly. We were a very proactive brothel, and we set so many standards in the industry. A customer could book an appointment with a lady for a particular date and time through our website. What a concept. Expedia.com had nothing on us! It was customary for Brenda to have appointments booked months in advance. Her specialty: couples. They loved her.

Her repeat clientele was endless. I remember speaking with one couple after they had a villa party with Brenda and they told me they planned their Las Vegas vacations around Brenda's schedule at the brothel. Can you believe it? People arranged their lives around these ladies. Who would have thought those dirty, little trailers would evolve into something like this?

Brenda probably is the one person I know who is just as crazy about animals as I am. She had two dogs and they were her children. When she would talk about her dogs, she would glow. One day Brenda came to my office, crying hysterically.

"Mom, I have to leave. My dog is hurt and I have to go."

"Calm down, honey. Go take care of your dog, but I don't want you driving in this condition. You have to calm down before I will give you your keys."

We collected the car keys from the ladies who drove themselves to the brothel. How hard would it be to stash drugs or money in their car, should they have access to it? So, we took their keys and if they did need something from their car, security would escort them and unlock their car for them. You have to think of everything.

Brenda calmed down, I gave her the keys and she left. I didn't charge her a fine for leaving early. This was a family emergency!

In general, though, should a lady leave before her scheduled departure date, she would be subject to quite a hefty fine. With such a large fine at stake, that discouraged them from leaving early. If they did leave early, it was a scheduling nightmare. I would try to find another lady who could book in, right now, and more often than not that wasn't happening.

Brenda called me a few hours later and sounded much better than the last time I had spoken with her. "Mom, it's Brenda. Everything is fine. Sparky just sprained his leg. Thank you, Mom, for everything."

Brenda stayed home with Sparky for the remainder of that week and came back to the brothel the following Monday. She had to see the doctor again to be tested for STDs and HIV. Every time a lady booked into the brothel, she was tested for STDs and HIV. She could be gone for as little as three days but it didn't matter. She was tested every time.

There was a stray cat that hung around the brothel that the ladies adopted. Brenda would buy the cat food, toys, a bed, you name it, and Brenda bought it all. I didn't mind having "Big Girl" (the cat) around, because she was cute and had so many caretakers. What a lucky cat! Anyhow, I thought it was appropriate. What would a cathouse be without a cat, right? If you couldn't find Brenda in the brothel, chances were she was in the courtyard playing with Big Girl.

A lot of the ladies would buy me a gift or give me a card for my birthday. Not Brenda. She would buy my dogs gifts for their birthdays. She just loved animals and so do I.

Whenever Brenda came to the brothel, the first thing out of my mouth was, "How are the babies?"

"They're so good, Mom, and how are all your babies?"

"Just fine, sweetheart." I have seven dogs — seven big dogs. Two St. Bernards, one pit, one German shepherd, one Dobie, one Newfoundland, and one golden Lab. That's my alternative to dieting. I just get bigger dogs! The bigger they are, the better I look!

Hattie

Hattie was unusual, to say the least, but you couldn't help but like her. Her thought processes were different than anyone's I ever met. Every conversation with Hattie began the same. You always felt like you just walked in on the middle of the conversation. It was typical for Hattie to see me and just start talking. "I knew I was right, Mom. That guy was wrong and I was right. Eagle feathers. I need eagle feathers."

"Hattie, what are we talking about?"

"Remember, Mom? That guy I partied with a couple of days ago. He was arguing with me that falcon feathers would bring me good luck and I told him, 'No, it's eagle feathers.' I was right, Mom, I knew I was right."

And then she would walk off, still carrying on the conversation, but this time with herself. After a while, you just got used to Hattie. It scared me a bit, but I found that as time passed, I actually knew what she was talking about without have to ask.

Needless to say, Hattie drove the other ladies crazy. She was constantly talking, and most times, they didn't know what she was talking about. But that never stopped Hattie. She just kept right on talking.

Hattie was older than most of the other ladies. She was in her forties, had three grown children and a grandchild on the way. She had curly, brown hair, pretty blue eyes and nonstop dialogue. Hattie had been in this line of work for more than twenty years. Her children were aware of what she did for a living and they didn't seem to mind. Hattie had a very close relationship with her children. She had been a single mom since her kids were small. Hattie did well. She supported her family comfortably and put all three of her children through college.

I remember one conversation with Hattie when she was telling me about her marriage. It seems her ex was a drug addict. She finally got tired of him hocking everything they owned to buy drugs and divorced him. I asked her if that was why she got into the business. She said: "No, I was a waitress in a restaurant when I was married and my plan was to keep working at the restaurant. I always made good tips, so there was no reason for me to leave."

"Then, why did you get into this business?" I asked.

"Well, Mom, you know, I was divorced and I wasn't getting any. That's why I got into the business. I needed to get some. Mom, I was so horny all the time, I couldn't stand it! Horny Hattie, that was me. But not no more. Now, I'm getting it ALL the time!"

Oh yeah, I forgot to mention that Hattie was a nymphomaniac. She couldn't get enough. Most of the ladies got into the business for the money, but not Hattie. She got into it for the sex. She just happened to get paid for it.

Hattie claimed she was from the northwest United States, but I would swear she was from Jupiter. I would guess they're all like her on her planet!

Kimmy

Kimmy was another of our more "mature" ladies. When I say "mature," I am referring to their age, not their behavior. Kimmy was in her very late forties. She was a beautiful blonde, although not a natural blonde. She had the biggest blue eyes you ever saw and a body you would die for. She looked like that in her late forties? I would have killed to have that body in high school!

A master of disguise, Kimmy had an array of wigs in all colors. Strawberry blonde, brunette, red, and black, and in all lengths and styles. She looked great in all of them. Kimmy had a perfectly shaped face with high cheekbones and the most beautiful smile you would ever see. She was gorgeous — nuts, but gorgeous.

Kimmy had a knack for disastrous relationships. You see, Kimmy wanted out of the business. After all, she was pushing fifty. She wanted desperately to find someone, anyone, and settle down in a "square life," as she called it. So, Kimmy fell in love with anyone she dated more than once. She would take off with these guys and follow them anywhere they went.

One day she called me from Texas, in tears.

"Mom, I can't believe it. Why do I believe everything these assholes tell me?"

It seemed Kimmy had followed yet another second date, this time to Texas. Supposedly he was in the oil business and had offered her half of his business for a not-so-nominal price. Well, Kimmy gave him the money and that was the last she saw of him. Stranded in Texas, she didn't know what to do, so she called me.

I can remember many conversations with Kimmy and most were basically the same. Now that I think about it, they were ALL the same. The only difference was the name of the guy. It wasn't that Kimmy was naïve, it was just that she so desperately wanted the "square life."

Kimmy always made good money, but it never failed: Every time she booked into the brothel, I would have to advance her the money for her doctor fees and sheriff's card. She would leave one week with a check for twenty thousand dollars and show up a week or two later broke. Dating Kimmy was the next best thing to winning the lottery.

Gisella

Gisella stood six feet tall without her high heels. She had blond hair, big boobs, and a great sense of humor. You had to know Gisella to appreciate her. The house was never quite the same when she wasn't there.

Not only did Gisella possess a quick wit, but she was extremely emotional. I can't remember too many conversations when I didn't hand her a tissue. We could be talking about the weather and she would cry. She expressed herself with such a passion that her tears would just flow. I think that is why she did so well at the brothel. The men she would negotiate with couldn't help but believe every word that came out of her mouth. No one could be that passionate and be lying, could they? She would tell them how handsome they were and what to expect should they spend some "quality" time with her. Although I could only hear the negotiations, I could just picture those guys sitting wide-eyed on the edge of her bed absorbing every word she spoke.

All negotiations were monitored for two reasons. First and foremost was for the safety and security of the ladies. Consider that you have a beautiful lady, scantily dressed, discussing sexual activities with a perfect stranger. I didn't want anyone getting overzealous during the negotiation process. Second, I always found that I slept much better at night knowing that when a lady booked a party for a thousand dollars, that a thousand dollars actually made it to the shift manager's desk. That was the second reason we monitored negotiations.

Gisella worked within every man's budget. Small parties, large parties, and everything in between. You would be hardpressed to leave the house, once you spoke to Gisella, and not share some quality time with her. She was a very hard lady to say no to.

Pampering was her specialty. She took the time to make every one of her customers feel like they were the only person who mattered. During the negotiation process, Gisella would massage their shoulders and neck until they were relaxed and carefree. After price and activity were agreed upon, Gisella would put on some soft music and offer her customer a drink from the bar. She would then scamper to the office with money in hand and entertain us while the shift manager booked her party.

"There was no way I was going to let this one get away. Grandma (as she always referred to herself) needs new boobs!" Gisella was in her forties and always referred to herself in the third person. She had a bubbly personality, that is, when she wasn't crying, and was an animal lover as well. She took over the care of Big Girl when Brenda wasn't at the brothel.

Being the animal lover that I am, I instituted a policy, when I began my employment at the brothel, of an "animal-friendly" environment. We didn't use any products in housekeeping, maintenance or any other departments that were tested on animals. Everything on the property was cruelty free. Gisella had a great appreciation for that policy.

Mia

Mia was a beautiful lady from Thailand who was in her mid-twenties. Mia had long, black hair and a petite build. Hell, I don't think she weighed a hundred pounds soaking wet. Mia was after the big bucks and didn't have a problem letting anyone know it. Whenever Mia was picked from a lineup or took a gentleman from the bar back to her room, the shift managers knew they needed to call another lady and have her "on deck." It wasn't unusual for Mia to "walk" her customer. After all, not everyone who showed up at the brothel had thousands of dollars . . . and that was all Mia was interested in.

A "walk" was defined as someone who went back to the room with a lady and negotiated but didn't reach an agreement on price and/or activity with the lady. We would then call another lady to speak with the customer. Our goal was always to keep all the money in the house. We never wanted any money to "walk" out of the house.

It wasn't unusual when Mia was picked from a lineup to have another lady or two hovering near the office so they could pick up her "walk." It got to the point where I had to implement a "Walk List" to keep it fair among the ladies. We would list any ladies, in alphabetical order, who were interested in picking up "walks." We would work our way down the list, with each walk going to the next lady on the list. Keeping an even playing field among the ladies was a priority.

Mia was another lady who referred to herself in the third person. Her negotiations were very entertaining, to say the least. "Honey, you don't like Mia? Mia likes you. Come on, honey, Mia wants to play with you. You want to play with Mia?" she would say in her strong Thai accent. Mia would persuade most of them, but some just didn't have enough money to spend on her. There would always be someone available to pick them up, though. It wasn't uncommon for any lady who picked up a walk from Mia to get a thousand, two thousand, even as much as three thousand dollars.

As I said, Mia was only interested in the big bucks. She supported her family in Thailand and sent the lion's share of her money back home. She worked regularly and would stay at the brothel for three weeks at a time, four weeks on occasion. She would only take five days off and then book right back in. Once a year she would leave for a month or two and go home to Thailand to visit her family.

Mia had a sweet personality, but you wouldn't want to get her mad. That Thai temper would kick in quick. When she was mad, she would talk at the rate of a thousand words per minute. The madder she got, the thicker her accent, and then try to figure out what she was saying! Good luck.

I would say to her, "Mia, slow down. What are you saying?" That would only make her more upset.

"Mom, aren't you listening to Mia?"

(You think it was easy being a madam? The only upside was, I never had to worry about identify theft. There wasn't anyone on this planet who wanted to be me!)

Christine

Christine was a tall, beautiful redhead who specialized in domination. She was in her late twenties, married, and had three children. You'd be surprised how many of the ladies were married with children. Their husbands were well aware of how they earned their money and had no problem with it. After all, someone had to pay for those million-dollar homes.

Everybody loved Christine. She had developed quite a following over the years and always had appointments any time she booked in to the brothel. She also was very popular with couples. Christine did it all . . . men, women, couples, but her favorite was domination. She referred to the dungeon (yes, we had a dungeon) as her "playground." She would take someone on a tour and show them the different party rooms we had to offer and when she got to the dungeon, she would say, "And this is my playground. In here I will make your ass as red as my hair." And she would. Guys couldn't get enough of it.

Dominance parties were a little different from "regular" parties. More often than not, there was no sexual activity in a dominance party. The domination activity took place in lieu of sexual activity. Since there was no sexual activity, the negotiations were a little different too. The customer and the lady would agree on a code word to be spoken during the party. Once this code word was spoken, the party was over. All the pleading in the world would not end the party, just the code word. Before entering the dungeon, the ladies would always remind the customer not to forget the code word, otherwise their punishment would never end.

When the dungeon was built, I hired a "dungeon master" to teach some of the ladies how to use all the implements properly. A good dominance session will leave you red and sore, but never bruised. You think it's easy to find a dungeon master? They're not in the Yellow Pages, you know.

I contacted the person who I purchased some of the dungeon equipment from. I met him at a porn convention. (What the hell has my life deteriorated to?) He gave me the name of a couple in California. They came to the brothel and seemed like nice enough people. He was a professor at one of the universities in California and his wife was a schoolteacher. By day they were teachers; by night they were dungeon masters! You just never know what people are into.

When I met them, they looked like teachers. When I saw them in the dungeon, he looked like Darth Maul from *Star Wars* and she looked downright evil. Their makeup and costumes were incredible.

They put on a two-hour demonstration in the dungeon and taught the ladies how to use the implements and how to talk to the customers. They covered everything: body language, tone of voice, technique. It was amazing to watch.

Christine was a natural. She was really into it and really good at it. It didn't take long before her reputation preceded her and most of her parties were dominance parties.

Once the lady and the customer entered the dungeon, the lady would be referred to as "Mistress" or "Ma'am" or however else the lady commanded the customer to address her.

The dungeon was the only party room that was monitored by the shift managers, sporadically, during a party. I needed to make sure that no one was screaming for their lives. It was very easy to get caught up in the moment in the dungeon. All customers were required to sign a release before using the dungeon.

"Please, Mistress, stop, I'll be good, I promise. Please, Mistress, you're hurting me," could be heard during these monitoring sessions. At that point, the mistress would smack them harder.

"No, *that* is hurting you. I was being nice before."

Christine was a master of dominance. She could beat the shit out of someone and never leave a bruise. Oh, they were red, quite red, but never a bruise. She would use wooden paddles, leather paddles, leather straps, cat-o'-nine tails, ball gags, handcuffs. She would lock them in cages, chain them to the wall. She did it all, and they loved every bit of it.

If the customer was into humiliation, after the party was over Christine would put a leash and collar on them and waltz them through the bar so everyone could see her work. The customer would wear a robe and Christine would make him bend over and lift up the robe to expose his well-beaten ass. Then she would smack him again. "Thank you, Mistress," he'd say, and they would walk off.

Oh well, just another day at the office!

Mary

Mary was our not-so-typical prostitute. Mary came to the brothel right after 9/11. Right after the tragedy in New York on September 11, 2001, the brothel business flourished. I don't know if everyone thought this might be the end of life as we knew it and wanted to get laid or what. I remember being glued to the TV in the bar with all the ladies and customers, watching the tragedy being aired over and over again. The ladies were sobbing, some of them uncontrollably. I would console them, one by one, as best I could. Hell, we were all scared, but I was their rock, and rocks don't get scared, right?

Anyway, shortly after 9/11, I got an e-mail from a beautiful lady from New York who wanted to come to work right away. That was Mary. She showed up at the brothel in a business suit, with one piece of luggage and her briefcase. Are you kidding me? Does she not know what a brothel is? I invited her into my office for a chat.

"Mary, are you sure you know what this type of work entails?"

"Yes, I am well aware this is a house of prostitution."

"You just don't seem to be the type, sweetheart."

"Well, I have to be. Actually, I am a marketing executive in New York City and I had a lot of investments in the stock market. I've lost a lot of money and I am trying to get my hands on some fast cash so I can salvage what I have left."

"Well, this is the place to do it."

At first it was rough for Mary. Her negotiations were very business-like. What a shock! I would speak with her customers, after they walked, and I would hear the same thing again and again, "I've never had an interview to get laid before." We would naturally find them another lady, but in the meantime, Mary needed help.

I would sit one on one with Mary and we would role-play negotiations. At first I would be Mary and she would be the customer, and then the reverse.

"Mary, you are a marketing executive. Use your marketing skills to market yourself. People are very visual; paint a picture of what type of experience you have in store for them. This is your area of expertise; use it to your advantage."

That piece of advice made Mary a lot of money. You see, once you put things in a perspective that people can relate to, the rest is easy.

Mary did fantastic. She did so fantastic that she gave up her marketing career and became one of our regular ladies.

Rochelle

Rochelle was an interesting addition to the brothel. She was in her early thirties, divorced and had one child. Rochelle had to have at least twelve different personalities. One time you would see her and she was as pleasant as she could be. Not five minutes later you would see her again and she was livid about something or other, ranting and raving. Then five minutes after that she would be solemn.

"Rochelle, is everything okay?"

"Fine," she'd reply and look at you as if you were crazy for asking.

For the most part, the other ladies steered clear of Rochelle, as did some of the staff. After a while, we would all learn to let Rochelle speak first. Then we would have a good idea of which personality we were dealing with, and we would adjust accordingly. It certainly made things interesting around the brothel.

Rochelle was a beautiful lady with big brown eyes and long brunette hair that lay across the middle of her back. Her smile took on whatever personality she possessed at the time. Sometimes it was sweet and sincere and other times it was just evil. She had a laugh that would echo throughout the hallways of the brothel. You ALWAYS knew when Rochelle was around.

There was one time when I was listening to her negotiation, which wasn't going too well. "You're not leaving this room, even if I have to stake you to the bed with my heels," she said to the customer. With that I heard him counting out hundred after hundred. Rochelle took the money and performed the DC.

"DC" was an industry term that stood for "Dick Check." The ladies would visually examine the gentleman's penis to make sure there was nothing irregular to prevent him from partying.

"I'll be right back, sweetheart." Sweetheart? She just threatened this guy and now he's "sweetheart"? That was Rochelle.

"Rochelle, do you really think it is necessary to threaten a customer?"

"It worked, didn't it?"

"Why don't you offer him a drink? I'm sure he could use one."

"He's got me. I'm intoxicating enough; he doesn't need a drink."

"Well, find out what he drinks. I'll send him one back from me."

"Okay." After the party, he couldn't thank me enough for that drink. I knew he needed one. I could have used one myself after listening to that negotiation.

Misha

Misha was a young, energetic con artist with dirty-blond hair. Misha could sell ice cubes to an Eskimo. She was about five feet four with a great body and an infectious laugh.

The highlight of Misha's day was mail call. She would get presents delivered on a daily basis — gifts from her customers, expensive ones. Every day was like Christmas for Misha. You wouldn't believe what would be delivered to the brothel for her. Computers (desktop and laptop), digital cameras, jewelry (from Tiffany and Cartier), designer purses, clothes, the latest and greatest cell phones, everything! Her taste was impeccable.

I remember when she was building her home, her million-dollar home. She had an 8,000-square-foot home built and she furnished the entire house with gifts from her customers. Misha really knew how to work her customers.

There was even a car delivered to the brothel for her. A Jaguar, naturally. Well, actually, it was two cars. The first one, a Corvette, showed up, but it was a stick shift. Misha didn't know how to drive a stick, so she gave it to another lady. She then let the customer know that she couldn't drive a stick so she gave it to a friend and he sent her the Jag. Unbelievable.

Her customers would ask her, "Can I tip you?"

"Of course you can. Send me a laptop. Send me a camera. Send me a car." And they would. She was amazing!

Jodie

I'll never forget the day Jodie called me.

"Is this the madam?"

"Yes, it is."

"Madam, I really need your help. I've been married for twenty years and my husband left me. I lost everything in the divorce. I don't have anything! I haven't worked in twenty years. I really don't have any skills, but I know I can do one thing . . . and I do it very well."

"E-mail me some photos, give me your phone number, and I'll call you as soon as I receive your pictures."

A few minutes later I received Jodie's e-mail. Not bad. Medium-length brunette hair, pretty face, and her body looked good.

I called Jodie back and booked her in. She was right about one thing: She didn't have anything, no clothes, no shoes, nothing. She showed up in jeans and a T-shirt and that was it. The ladies actually were pretty compassionate. They took her back to one of their rooms and played "dress-up" with Jodie. Before long, Jodie had ten or so outfits.

She had her STD/HIV tests done and the next day Fernando took her to the Sheriff's Department to get her sheriff's card. So was so excited and couldn't wait to start working.

Jodie was picked out of the first lineup she was in. During her dress-up session, the other ladies gave her pointers on how to negotiate. The ladies would be helpful, at times, with the new ladies. It all depended on their moods. Luckily for Jodie, they were in an obliging mood when she arrived.

Jodie was forty-five years old when she came to the brothel. It never failed — every time she booked back in and saw me, she would say: "Mom, I should have done this years ago. I have more today than I had in my twenty years of marriage."

It wasn't long before Jodie bought a house, a car, a wardrobe to die for, and all the things she wanted. She had no desire to get remarried. Hell, she had life by the horns. Her children were grown and had no idea what she was doing. They were busy with their lives and she visited them whenever she wanted to. She didn't have to explain anything to anyone anymore. She loved her new independence and her new life.

Chandrell

Chandrell was a beautiful young girl from the islands. She was twenty-three years old and actually had some college education. Chandrell came to the brothel the year she turned twenty-one. She wanted to make some extra money during her summer break from college and that's how she wound up at the brothel. She had long brown hair, a petite build, and she was a wild one. She loved rap music, and every night in the bar it was like a sorority party when Chandrell was in the house.

One day she came running into my office in tears.

"Mom, what am I going to do?"

"What's the problem, honey?"

"It's my parents. They want to know when I am going to graduate."

You see, Chandrell supposedly had been in college for six years, but for the past three she had been working in the brothel. She made so much money the first summer that she didn't see the need to go back to school.

"I make more money doing this than I would with my degree," she told me.

I tried to persuade her to go back to school, but at twenty-three Chandrell couldn't see the big picture. All she could see was that she was making ten thousand dollars a week, on average, and with a degree in nursing, she could never make that much.

Chandrell never told her parents she had quit college and apparently she kept the money her parents had sent her for her schooling.

"I can't tell them what I'm doing, they'll kill me!" she cried. "What am I going to do? I know, I'll tell them I changed my major. That should buy me another year or so, won't it, Mom?"

"Chandrell, you can't keep taking the money your parents are sending you for school. You have to tell them you left school."

She eventually told her parents that she had left college and was working on a cruise ship, which gave her the latitude she needed to be away from home for extended periods. Her parents weren't happy, I'm sure.

Chandrell worked at the brothel for four more years. After she retired, she did complete her college education and is now working part-time as a nurse for "extra money."

Her family never did find out that she worked at the brothel.

Lillian

Lillian stood only five feet tall without her heels. She was the tiniest thing, with long, straight, blond hair, naturally blond. Lillian had such a sweet smile and the softest voice you would ever hear. She was like a little Barbie doll. Lillian had a great body, petite with big, big boobs. When people would see her they would do a double-take. When they found out she was older than fifty, had five kids, and was a grandmother, they would do a triple-take. Can someone actually look that good after five kids? Lillian did.

Lillian was married and her husband knew what she did for a living. He worked in Las Vegas and they had a fantastic marriage. He would help out with the kids and the grandkids when she was at the brothel.

The customers loved her. Lillian had pictures of her kids and grandkids all around her room. Customers would ask about the pictures, and Lillian would answer, "These are my sons, these are my daughters, and these are my grandkids." They would be blown away. We were all blown away.

Lillian had quite a following. Her customers could relate to her. She was a real person with a real family who went through the same day-to-day problems we all went through with marriage and kids. You would think this would be a turn-off to most people; after all, they come to the brothel to escape their everyday lives. But Lillian's customers loved it. And when they found out her husband knew what she did for a living and was supportive of her occupation, that excited them even more. I guess there would be some sense of excitement, for some, knowing that you're sleeping with another man's wife and he was okay with it.

Lillian would share stories of her personal life with her customers, which was highly unusual in the business. Most of the ladies were very secretive about their personal lives and that's why they used "floor names," not their real names. Just like strippers use "stage names," the ladies of the brothel used "floor names." They could be anyone they wanted to be.

Ladies choose to work in this profession for a variety of reasons. Most people think they are victims of abuse and abandonment. Although, unfortunately, many of them are, there are just as many who aren't.

I can remember a countless number of ladies who were abused by family members during their childhood. Not only sexual abuse, but physical abuse, verbal abuse, and drug abuse. There were even ladies who had been addicted to alcohol in their infancy. It is hard to imagine, but these things really do take place. A lot of the ladies came out of these types of horrific environments.

There was one lady who was absolutely beautiful. Her name was Shane. She had just turned twenty-one when she came to the brothel. But mentally, Shane was about twelve. She was so childlike. Her mother was a crackhead who would force liquor down her throat as a baby. When Shane got a little older, her mother would put her in bed with her boyfriend of the moment. She would use Shane as a tool and offer sexual favors from Shane to an endless number of men to support her crack habit. This went on until Shane was eighteen years old.

How sad was that? For the past three years, Shane had been living on the streets and was waiting to turn twenty-one so she could work at the brothel. The story just broke my heart. How could anybody do something like that to a child, their own child, no less? What kind of world do we live in? People are quick to judge prostitution: It's immoral, it's despicable, it's dirty. I've heard them all. In Shane's case, she was lucky there was such a thing as legal prostitution. It provided her with a safe haven. No more abuse. She was taken care of when she got sick, she wasn't alone anymore, she had someone to turn to — she finally had a mom.

Anyone can give birth. It really doesn't take a lot of talent. But not just anyone can be a mom. And the really sad part was, Shane wasn't the only one who had such a tumultuous childhood. There were many more. I suppose it is easier to look the other way. If you don't see it, it doesn't exist. But I know, firsthand, it does. I've seen the products of those horrible childhoods, and I've seen those children flourish once they found something, someone who would protect them and love them. It was almost as if the brothel had given them a second lease on life. Surely, that couldn't be despicable, could it?

The ladies came from all walks of life. They came from good homes with loving families, from broken homes, and there were those who grew up in foster homes. There were ladies who had college degrees and those with no more than an elementary school education. They ranged from executives to street walkers and everything in between. Then there were the ladies, like Mary, who were trying to get out of a financial bind.

They ranged in age from twenty-one to fifty-plus. Different economic backgrounds, different social backgrounds; different cultural backgrounds, different religious backgrounds. The United Nations had nothing on us! We had almost every country represented at one time or another.

Customers were intrigued with the ladies who had foreign accents. One time we had ladies in the house from ten different countries. A customer came in and was talking with them in the bar. He partied with each of the ten ladies. As he left he couldn't stop raving about the great time he had. "I felt like I took a trip around the world!" he said. The only thing missing were the frequent flier miles, I suppose.

There were a lot of ladies who worked in the brothel just for a specific amount of time. They had goals of how much they wanted to earn or needed to earn, and once they reached their goal, they got out of the business. One lady in particular who had such a goal was Mackenzie. She was twenty-two when she came to the brothel. She had long blond hair, green eyes, and a perfect body. She wanted to make as much money as she could in five years. Then it was her plan to retire. And that's exactly what Mackenzie did.

During her five-year tenure, she owned a $3 million home in one state, a $2 million condo in another, and a $1 million loft in yet another state. She retired five years later with more money than she would ever need and no one would ever know what she had been doing to earn her living. At twenty-seven Mackenzie retired.

The ladies didn't finance anything. They paid cash. What they had, they owned. The ladies, who were independent contractors, paid their taxes just like the rest of us working stiffs. But unlike most of us, they lived lives of luxury. They lived in showcase homes, drove Maseratis, Lamborghinis, Bentleys, Mercedes, nothing but the best.

I remember one day I was walking through the dining room of the brothel and I saw Kathy wearing the cutest shoes. "I love those shoes, Kathy."

"Oh, Mom, I got them on sale. They were only six hundred dollars."

Six hundred dollars! I didn't know they made shoes for six hundred dollars!

"Do you want me to pick a pair up for you, Mom?"

"No thank you, sweetheart. I never had to finance a pair of shoes before and I'm not going to start now."

"Oh, Mom, you're so funny!"

Chapter Eight

MEET THE CUSTOMERS

The customers were an interesting bunch. We got everything from your everyday businessman to, well, the more unconventional types. Where does one begin? Let's start with the Good Humor man. Remember the ice cream man who used to drive around the neighborhood on hot summer days? You know, the guy in the white pants and white shirt driving the ice cream truck and ringing the bell? Well, the brothel had its own version of the Good Humor man. He was middle-aged, average height, average weight, but not your average party. He wasn't interested in sexual activity. He could get that from his wife. What he wanted was to make banana splits on the ladies and lick them off of them. I had to make sure we had all the fixings so as not to ever disappoint the Good Humor man. Rubber sheets were a must. We didn't want all that gooey stuff soaking into the mattresses. He would pay a pretty good price to turn one of the ladies into a banana split. We had it all: strawberry, vanilla, and chocolate ice cream, strawberry and chocolate syrups, bananas, of course, whipped cream, and cherries. I'm sure you can picture where the cherry was placed.

We would deliver all the ingredients to the room and he would begin to prepare his banana split. The lady would lay naked on her back on top of the rubber sheets. He would then proceed to strategically place ice cream scoops on her body. After all the ice cream scoops were put in place, he followed with the syrups, the bananas, the whipped cream, and at last, the cherry! He would devour his banana split, licking away to his heart's content. Afterward, he and the lady would shower and that was his party. Talk about your ice cream social!

And who could forget our lumberjack ballerina? This was a big, burly lumberjack sort of fellow. Red, curly, shoulder-length hair and a red, scraggly, full beard. He would come into the bar dressed in a pink, ruffled tutu and pink ballet slippers. Oh, he was a sight to see. He would order a beer and mingle with the ladies. At first you couldn't take your eyes off him, but after a while, we all got used to him. As time progressed, he really didn't look that odd to us. What was this job doing to me? Who would ever believe that a lumberjack in a pink tutu wouldn't seem odd?

Then there was the guy who dressed as a woman and would come in to party with one of our big bookers. This guy was a regular at the brothel. I knew him as a guy but when he came up to the counter to pay for his party (he insisted on coming to the counter as he wanted as many people to see him as possible), he actually looked better as a woman. It was more than just wigs and makeup, it was the whole package: high heels, garter belt and stockings, bra and panties, tight-fitting dress covering her (or his) extra-large breasts, jewelry. He was definitely a fashion statement. This guy knew how to accessorize! He dressed better than some of my staff members.

Of course there were the ordinary fetishes: foot fetishes, smoking fetishes (guys who wanted the ladies to smoke during sex), golden showers, you know, your average kinks. But there were quite a few strange ones, too.

One guy would pay the ladies to stomp on him with their high heels. He would strip naked and lie on the floor. The lady would wear nothing but her six-inch heels and stomp the hell out of him. He would start out lying on his stomach and then roll over on his back and she would stomp him all over again. This guy was nuts — yes, they would stomp them too. Ouch!

There were quite a few customers who wanted the ladies to use a "strap-on" on them. A strap-on is a dildo fastened to a belt that the lady would wear around her waist. She would then perform anal sex on the customer. Let me tell you, these were no petite dildos, they were huge! The bigger they were, the better the customers liked them. And the ladies, well, they weren't exactly gentle. They slammed them as hard as they could. We were all about customer satisfaction. Even when dildos were used in a party, a condom was put on the dildo. The ladies really enjoyed those types of parties. One guy spent so much for one of these parties that he asked me if I would comp him the strap-on from the gift shop. "It would be my pleasure," I said. I remember my casino days when I used to comp dinners. Now I was comping dildos!

We had our share of guys who were into humiliation. They would insist that the ladies verbally abuse them and smack them around a bit. It wasn't a dominance party, because they wanted to have sex. They just wanted to be degraded while having sex. Then they would pay other ladies to come in during the party for some more verbal abuse and to criticize their performance. Just what you want during sex . . . a critic.

One guy who was into humiliation insisted that after his party was over, he wanted to be kicked down the hallway, through the parlor, and out the front door. He was on his hands and knees as the lady kept booting his ass all the way down the hallway, right out the parlor door. We aimed to please!

There were quite a few mothers or fathers who would bring in their sons when they turned twenty-one. In speaking with the parents, their reasoning for bringing their son to the brothel was quite simple. They wanted their son's first experience with a woman to be a good one, so they came to us. Any twenty-one-year-old who came to the brothel with his mom or dad was a virgin. Go figure. I always thought it was refreshing to know there were still twenty-one-year-old virgins running around.

The parent would pay for his son's party and would sit and talk to me while the son was "busy." I heard it so many times: "It is important to us to know that his first experience with a woman is a good experience for him. I'm so glad there are places like this where he can go and be with a professional. We want him to know how to please a lady and know how to treat a lady." You have to admire a parent like that. All the time I was listening to the parents, I was thinking that if I had brought my son to a brothel when he turned twenty-one, I would have been quite a few years too late!

The ladies loved having virgins. They would come out of those parties all excited and bubbly. They loved to teach men how to please a woman. The ladies were very sincere and gentle with them and they would spend more time with a virgin than they normally would with other parties. Surprisingly, we got quite a lot of virgins at the brothel, and they were so grateful. They would come out of the room wide-eyed and grinning. I'm sure those grins remained on their faces long after their party was over.

Customers could spend as little as $200 at the brothel, but sexual intercourse would not be part of the deal. For that amount, the customer would receive a quick bout of oral sex or, more likely, stimulation by hand. Although our brothel sold activity, not time, for $200 that activity wouldn't take very long. The ladies were masters of making someone feel like a million bucks within a ten- to fifteen-minute window. Just as customers would come to the brothel for different reasons, their budgets were just as different. I remember one customer had just inherited quite a large amount of money. He stayed at the brothel for more than a month and spent almost half a million dollars. He really loved the ladies and, believe me, the ladies loved him.

One gentleman, a very wealthy man from a neighboring state, took a limousine to the brothel. At the time he arrived, I had twenty-four ladies in the house. He was a very good-looking man, well spoken, wearing a Rolex Presidential watch, a diamond pinky ring, and an expensive suit. I welcomed him at the door.

"Would you like a lineup? I asked.

"I certainly would," he replied.

Our lineup was gorgeous and I could see he was pleased with what we had to offer.

"Well, have you made a decision?" I asked.

"Yes, I have, I would like all of your ladies!"

"All of them?" I asked just to clarify that I heard him correctly.

"Madam, do you think I could party with all of them, three at a time?"

"I don't see why not."

He picked the first three ladies and off they went to negotiate. He stayed at the brothel for twenty-six hours, partied with twenty-four ladies, and spent a ton of money. He tipped each lady very generously and tipped all of the staff as well. As he was leaving, I asked if we would see him again.

"I can't thank you enough for giving me the time of my life. I enjoyed this day more than any other day. I'd like to say that I will be back but unfortunately I cannot. You see, I'm dying. I don't have much time left and I wanted to take something with me to remember. Thank you for the memory."

As I watched him get into his limousine, I was overcome with mixed emotions. I was sad to hear that he was dying. He was such a nice man. By the same token, I was glad that we were able to give him what he came for: a memory that he could take with him. I don't know how much time he had left, but I did know that the smile on his face would last as long as he would.

When people think of brothels, they think of "sex for money". Not all the activities at the brothel consisted of sex. We had many men, particularly elderly men, come to the brothel, have a line-up, pick a lady and his party consisted of nothing more than talking; that's it . . . just talking.

These men had been married to the same woman for many, many years. Their wife had pre-deceased them and they found themselves alone. Their children were grown and were busy with children of their own. Their children were often busy with soccer games, school plays and everything else that young families' lives revolve around. They didn't have the time to dedicate to their surviving parent; time they desperately needed. When you spend the majority of your life with someone and you get left behind, you don't feel "whole" anymore. A part of you has been put to rest, right along with your spouse.

So they came to us. They would come to us seeking nothing more than companionship. They wanted someone to listen to their stories. Stories about a new garden they had planted perhaps; stories about an old friend they had heard from; stories about how much they missed their wife. They wanted someone to share a piece of their life with, even if it was only temporary. They would hold hands with the Lady and reminisce of how they missed the touch of a woman.

So you see, brothels are not always about sex; they are about companionship, about sharing, about easing someone's loneliness; even if it was only temporary.

Men would come to the brothel and fall in love with a lady. They would want to rescue the lady, trying to convince her that she didn't need to do what she was doing, that she could leave with him and would be taken care of. The ladies had a hard time trying to convince these men that they didn't want or need to be rescued. They loved what they did. Most customers couldn't understand that the intimate moments they had spent with a lady were no more than a business transaction for the lady.

A number of customers would stalk the ladies. There was one guy who made contact with a lady's mother. The lady made the grave mistake of telling her customer her real name. This was taboo in the industry. For the most part, the ladies never revealed their true identities. They had to protect themselves from situations just like this.

Some men would follow the ladies when they left the brothel, trying desperately to persuade them to abandon the life they were leading. They just couldn't understand that the ladies had chosen their profession. Nor could they understand that most of them couldn't afford to take care of the ladies in the manner to which they were accustomed. These ladies were used to the best of everything. They made a lot of money, and if they didn't have a pimp or a family, they spent it all on themselves. They were high maintenance! I don't know how many times I would have to intervene, on the ladies' behalf, and speak with gentlemen who were on a rescue mission.

Just when I thought I'd seen and heard it all, I received a phone call from a couple who wanted to have their wedding at the brothel. A wedding here? It seemed they were into the dominance thing and wanted to have a "collaring" ceremony in the dungeon. Why not?

"We want the ladies to participate in the ceremony. After we exchange our wedding vows, we want the ladies to strip us, chain us to the wall, and have their way with us." Okay, so this wasn't your average "fairy tale" wedding.

We did it. They actually found a minister who agreed to perform the ceremony for them. I'm sure it was a first for this minister. How many collaring ceremonies in a brothel do you think he had performed before this one? Right after they said, "I do," he left. Smart man. The poor guy is probably still in therapy.

Now it was time for the post-nuptial activities to begin. I've got to tell you, considering what they spent on this wedding, they could have had a gala affair at the Ritz. They paid all the ladies to dominate them. Two ladies at a time would go into the dungeon. It became a contest among the ladies as to who could administer the best domination session. I was just hoping that by the time the last two ladies finished their work, our newlyweds were still alive.

Well, they lived through it and couldn't have been happier. They thanked me over and over for making their wedding day the most special day of their lives. You see, it takes all kinds to make up this crazy world we live in. To see this couple, you wouldn't think they were any different from anyone you may pass on the street. But get them behind closed doors and watch out! It's those little idiosyncrasies that make us all individuals, I guess. The ladies were all excited too. "Mom, that was the most fun we've had in a long time!" It's the simple pleasures that make life precious.

We had our regulars who just came to drink at the bar. One local guy would come into the bar every day after he got off work. He would have his usual two beers and dinner. He always sat on the same barstool, right at the corner of the bar. And if someone happened to be sitting in his stool when he came in, let me tell you, he was not a happy camper. We tried to make sure his stool was available for him — sometimes we were successful, other times we weren't. He was never interested in partying. He just enjoyed coming in after a day's work, having a beer or two, maybe some dinner, and socializing with the ladies. During football season, he was there every Monday night for the game. The ladies loved sitting and talking with him and never minded that he didn't want to party.

Our local bar clientele got to know the ladies quite well and developed a rapport with them. They enjoyed the ladies' conversations and company. Why not? The ladies were charming and witty in addition to their beauty. They were no different from other women. Many of our local bar customers were surprised at first by these qualities that the ladies possessed. I'm not sure what people may have thought about prostitutes, but I know they never thought of them as "regular" people, not until they met them anyway.

And our local clientele was extremely important to the brothel. They were voters! Whether they partook in brothel services wasn't important. What was important was that they knew what the brothels were all about and they knew the people who worked in those brothels. The brothel employees were people just like you and me. Imagine that.

There were guys who just came in to shoot pool with the ladies. One of our ladies, Laura, was quite the pool shark. I don't think she ever lost a game. You don't suppose her straddling the pocket the guy was shooting for, in her g-string, would be considered cheating, do you?

The bar wasn't like a strip club. There was no pressure, no hard sales pitch. It was just a neighborhood bar that happened to be populated by beautiful, half-naked women. You didn't have to partake in brothel services to hang out in the bar. It became quite a popular place for the locals to meet, have a drink, and enjoy the scenery.

Chapter Nine

RED HATS, BIKERS, AND CELEBS

I was in my office one day when I received a phone call from an older lady. "I belong to a group and we want to have lunch someplace different and I thought your place would be fun."

"Well, we're certainly different. How many in your group?"

"There are thirty of us."

Hmmm, thirty little old ladies. That should be interesting.

"Let me tell you what we can do. We can put a buffet lunch together for your group and then give the group a tour after lunch. How does that sound?"

"That sounds wonderful."

So, I put a nominally priced buffet together for them and we did it: our first group tour. Little did I know this would be the first of many.

The following Wednesday, the kitchen set up a buffet in the bar before the little old ladies arrived at eleven-thirty. They were all dressed in purple and red. What kind of group was this? The Red Hat Society.

The Red Hats, I came to find out, were a social group for women fifty and older. I had never heard of the Red Hats before, but as time passed I would learn a lot about them. They were just adorable, all dressed up in purple and red. They wore red hats of every shape and size and decorated to match each respective owner's personality. How fun! The Red Hats were enjoying their lunch and the ladies were enjoying the Red Hats. They had a ball answering their questions. After lunch I took the Red Hats on a tour.

We started in the parlor. I introduced myself and handed each of them my business card. "I couldn't help but notice how beautiful you all are, and should you be looking for a career change, I would appreciate you calling me personally." They laughed. I showed them all the different amenity rooms and explained to them how the brothel worked. It never failed that no matter what type of group we had come through, the dungeon was where we spent the most time and they had the most questions. They had so many great questions. They were genuinely interested in how everything worked.

Next stop: the villas. We toured each available villa. If a villa was in use during a tour, I would explain to the group that the villa was "busy," but if they were interested in paying for a "voyeur party," I would be happy to show it to them. Again, they laughed.

Our first tour was a huge success. The tour ended where it began: in the parlor. One by one, each Red Hat shook my hand and thanked me for such a wonderful tour.

"I had no idea that these places were so nice."

"Your ladies are just divine."

"The ladies are so sweet and friendly."

"I think prostitution should be legal everywhere."

"To tell you the truth, I wasn't too crazy about coming to a brothel, but you sure changed my way of thinking."

"I've learned so much, thank you."

Everyone had a great time, but more importantly, I learned something, too. We were changing perceptions about brothels.

From that day forward, we offered luncheons and tours to groups and organizations. I had a "group tour" section added to our website. The Red Hats were our best promoters. I never realized how many different chapters of The Red Hat Society there were. There were more than one hundred in Las Vegas alone and fourteen chapters just in the little town of Pahrump.

We had so many Red Hat groups tour the brothel that I had special T-shirts and coffee mugs made for them. "Where the Red Hats meet the Red Lights"; they loved them. Of course, the T-shirts and mugs were purple, with red lettering and our logo. I couldn't keep them in stock. They told everyone about their brothel tours. Before I knew it, we had tours booked almost every day of the week.

We had many different groups tour the brothel. The Shriners, City of Hope, planning commissions, law enforcement groups, chief petty officer groups — the list went on and on. Then tour companies from Las Vegas started calling to ask if we could put something together for their groups as well. Sure, why not? We had buses come to the brothel full of curious people of all types. No matter what type of group toured the brothel, the comments were pretty much the same. They raved about how clean it was, how beautiful and friendly the ladies were, and how nice the staff was. But most of all, we changed their way of thinking. We changed thousands of perceptions over the years. It's something that would help us later on.

It didn't end with tours. That was just the beginning. We started hosting car shows and biker runs. We even had a benefit for the Vietnam veterans. It was like being in the casino all over again. Who would have thought I'd be hosting events at a brothel?

The brothel became a frequent stop on biker poker runs. Those were a lot of fun. One Saturday, I'll never forget it, we inadvertently double-booked events. We had a biker poker run in the morning and a Red

Hat luncheon and tour in the afternoon. Oh, this was going to be interesting.

The bikers started pulling in to the brothel about ten o'clock in the morning. They ordered a beer and got their poker card from the bartender. The ladies loved mingling with the bikers and the bikers loved it even more. The bikers tended to stay a little longer at the brothel than they did at other stops on the run. Imagine that.

At eleven-thirty I saw a bus full of Red Hats pull into the parking lot, which was packed with motorcycles. The bar was filled with bikers. I went out to meet the bus. I got on the bus and welcomed the Red Hats.

"Hello, ladies. We have a biker poker run today, but don't worry, we have you all set up for lunch in the dining room."

I feared those little, old ladies would have a collective nervous breakdown when they saw all those motorcycles. Boy was I wrong. They were climbing all over the motorcycles, getting their pictures taken on the bikes, taking pictures with the bikers. They were having a blast. When they walked into the bar, dolled up in their purple and red outfits with those magnificent red hats, the bikers all turned and looked at them.

"Hello, boys! We're the second shift," announced one of the Red Hats.

You should have seen it! Big, burly bikers and those sweet, little Red Hats. It couldn't have worked out any better if it were planned.

The bikers were never a problem. There was a stigma about them — sort of like brothels, not very flattering. We welcomed them. Who were we to judge anybody? I knew exactly how they felt. There would be times when people wouldn't even take my business card.

I remember when my husband and I went on our first cruise. You know how cruises are. You are seated with the same people for dinner every night. Everyone introduces themselves and idle conversations begin.

"Where are you from?"

"We're from Las Vegas."

"Vegas! Do you work in a casino?"

"I used to."

"What do you do now?"

"I work in the hospitality industry."

"Where?"

"Just outside of Las Vegas."

They would keep asking questions and I would do my best to avoid being specific. But if they kept pushing the envelope, finally I would tell them what I did.

"So, you're a madam?"

"I am."

There would be one of two reactions. Either I would not see them again for the remainder of the cruise or they would be so curious, they would ask a million questions. The curious people, after a few moments of conversation, would begin to talk to me about their sex lives; particularly the men. It never failed. They would share with me their fantasies, auspicious encounters they had, and sexual fantasies they would like to have. They would be very detailed and graphic, leaving nothing to the imagination. As they spoke, I would have visuals of what they were describing running through my head. Oh, please stop! Do you know how hard it was trying to have a conversation with these people, trying to be polite while they were going on and on about their sex lives? Did they think I really gave a shit?

I was a madam, not a sex therapist. When I met a plumber, I didn't start telling him about my faucets. I never told a chef about my cooking or told a builder about my home. Why would someone share something so personal with a stranger who just happened to be a madam? I suppose people assumed that since I was a madam, I was some sort of sexual liberal. I suppose they assumed that madams were very open and public about sex. I suppose they assumed that if you were a madam, you must be some sort of sexual deviant. They couldn't grasp that it was a job.

The brothels were under constant scrutiny, but we were gaining popularity in the community. We were the only brothel at the time that invited the public in. No strings attached, come on by and check it out. Everyone was curious about the brothels and we satisfied their curiosity. As long as you were twenty-one, you were welcome at our brothel.

We hosted a fundraising event for a biker group, a member of which had been diagnosed with a terminal illness and had no insurance. They came to me and asked if we would help. We did. It was a local biker group and I was glad that the brothel could assist and even happier that they thought of us when they needed help. I met with several of the group's leaders and together we planned the event.

"There's going to be a lot of different colors here at this event, but usually they are pretty good at these types of things."

Usually? What the hell does that mean? "They're not going to kill one another, are they?" I asked.

"Let's hope not."

That was comforting. "No one is allowed to bring any type of weapons on the property," I informed them.

"We'll let them know. We have our own security. I know the brothel has security, but we will have our own as well. Bikers tend to listen to other bikers better than other people."

Great.

I think every biker club west of the Rockies came to the fundraising event. I'd never seen so many bikers in one place before, and as luck would have it, they were at my place. I have to admit I was a little nervous. We had a band, food, drinks, and, of course, beautiful ladies. I thought everything was going well until one of the leaders I had met with to organize this thing came to me and said, "We may have a little problem."

I'm thinking to myself that a "little problem" to these guys has got to include a body count. "No one is dead, are they?"

"No. But one of the Hell's Angels won't give up his gun."

Hell's Angels, are you kidding me?

"So, I thought you might talk to him."

"What happened to bikers listening to other bikers?" I asked.

"Well, I spoke to him, but he won't give up his gun. Maybe you can talk to him."

Sure, why not. That's my area of expertise, disarming a Hell's Angel. This night couldn't end quickly enough.

He pointed out the Hell's Angel to me in the bar and off I went. All of a sudden I felt like I was "Walking the Green Mile."

"Excuse me, sir. Can I talk to you? Let's walk outside where it is a little quieter."

What the hell was I thinking? If he shoots me, at least there should be a witness, shouldn't there? Good thinking, take him somewhere where there is no one around. Brilliant.

"What's your name?"

"Jack."

"Jack, I'm the madam and we have a policy in effect which does not allow any type of weapons on the property."

"Well, I am the sergeant at arms and I am never without my weapon."

"I appreciate that, Jack . . . Sergeant, but we're governed by some pretty strict statutes and I am going to have to ask you either to leave your weapon with your bike or you will have to leave the property."

I could see that Jack was a little irritated and I figured he was going to shoot me right about then. Jack said, "I'm the sergeant at arms; you don't seem to understand that."

"I do and I appreciate your position. However, on this property you are outranked, Sergeant."

Jack was silent for a moment and then said, "Do you have a place where you can lock up my gun?"

"Sure, we can lock it up in the safe. Follow me."

I placed Jack's gun in the safe and then I asked him, "Do any of your guys have weapons on them?"

"Yes."

Of course, what was I thinking? "I would appreciate you having your guys remove their weapons from the property."

"No problem, I'll take care of it. Can I tell you something?" Jack asked.

"Sure."

"You've got balls," he said. "I like you; you've got some balls."

We laughed, and then Jack rounded up his guys and their weapons. Sure, I got balls . . . no brains, but balls!

Our clientele was diverse, to say the least. When people think about the individuals who visit a brothel, they think of guys who can't get laid any other way. As you now have some idea, that couldn't be farther from the truth. How many other establishments could you go to that catered to such a wide range of customers, from bikers to the royal family, and everything in between?

Oh sure, we had royalty visit and partake from time to time. That was a unique experience. Guards were posted outside the lady's room. I had to sign confidentiality agreements. The lady or ladies who were chosen had to sign confidentiality agreements. Who would have thought there would be so much paperwork just to get laid?

Celebrities would fly in by helicopter. High-profile clients would land in the courtyard and would be brought in through the back of the brothel. The brothel industry was a very discreet business and we would go to great lengths to preserve that discretion. Clients varied from musicians to athletes to movie stars.

You could always tell when a high-profile client was in the house: The ladies would tend to argue more than usual. Naturally that would all take place in the back of the house, so the client was never aware of the chaos he was creating among the ladies. Do you remember how girls would fight over the cutest guy in the class? It was like high school all over again. At times I would just sit back in my chair in my office and laugh. It was like running an X-rated day care. If the ladies didn't make things interesting enough, I knew I could always count on the customers to pick up the slack.

Chapter Ten

Let's Party!

To celebrate the completion of the new brothel and all it had to offer, I decided to throw a big party — your typical party, not a brothel-type party. Alert the media! We'll invite everyone, radio stations, TV stations, newspapers, the town of Pahrump, Las Vegas . . . everyone. So I began planning, putting together the VIP list, collecting addresses for the invitations.

The invitations. I have to design an invitation. Something sexy, yet not offensive. It has to be classy. After all, this isn't just any party. No, this will be an event!

We'll have it in the summer, out in the courtyard. Perfect. We'll put up tents, a stage for the band. Have to find a band — add that to the list. We'll have to get tables and chairs, but for how many? What if no one shows up? No brothel had ever thrown a party before, much less an event. I'd thrown hundreds of parties in the past and every one was a success. I'd hate to ruin a perfect record. Maybe I shouldn't . . . oh, what the hell, we're doing it. Positive thinking.

I designed a classy and sexy invitation and ordered one thousand of them. Now that's positive thinking. Of course people would come. Who wouldn't want to be invited to an event at a brothel? If nothing else, just to satisfy their curiosity, right? It doesn't matter who you are, male or female, married or single, straight or bi, everyone has a genuine curiosity about brothels. After all, they're so mysterious and intriguing, and not everyone has the opportunity to ever see one. This was going to be great!

I was busy making lists. Lists of things to order, lists of things to buy, lists of people, lists of addresses. You name it, there was a list for it. Santa had nothing on me.

It took three months of planning. The invitations were sent out a month before the event. I gave the shift managers a list (yet another list) for any RSVPs they might receive. I placed an ad in the newspapers inviting everyone to our event. Tickets could be purchased at the brothel for those who weren't on the VIP list. It was too late to turn back now.

I decided to close the gift shop inside and move it out to the courtyard for our event. We'll set up a retail tent and make a killing!

Invitations were sent out to all the radio stations, television stations, newspapers, our regular brothel customers, the Queen Mothers of the numerous Red Hat groups that had toured the brothel, politicians, casino hosts, and casino general managers.

I knew the minute the invitations were delivered. Disc jockeys from the various radio stations were calling the brothel and wanting to speak with the madam, on the air, about the event. It was great. I spoke with all the different radio personalities about our event. Then their listeners started calling in and asking questions. The publicity we were getting was incredible . . . and, better yet, it was free! Since at that time brothels were not permitted, by law, to advertise, this was a wonderful thing for us. We weren't advertising; we were simply talking about the event.

One of the radio stations asked if we would give them two tickets to the event to be used as the grand prize for a contest.

"Sure, why not." Even more publicity!

The RSVPs were starting to come in. I checked the RSVP lists every day, although the shift managers swore I checked them every ten minutes.

The festivities would include food, drinks, live entertainment, dancing under the stars, drawings for gifts, tours of the brothel, and the chance to mingle with the most beautiful women you would ever see. The event would be held in the evening when the desert sun began to set. Yes, at sunset. What a beautiful backdrop that would be. Perfect!

I remember sitting on my patio having coffee with my husband one morning before work and we were talking about the event. I was rattling off all my plans to him. We're going to have tents and a stage and a band and . . .

"What about power?" he asked.

"Power? What power?"

"It's at night, right? You're going to need power for lights under the tents, power to the stage for lighting and equipment. Power. What about power?"

"I don't have any power! What am I going to do? People are coming, they RSVP'd!"

The event is less than two weeks away and I don't have power. What an idiot! It wasn't on any of my lists!

"Calm down. I'll call James and see if he can come out and help me run some power. Do you have any outlets outside?"

"No."

The following Saturday, my husband and James came out to the brothel.

"How many amps does the band need?"

"What?"

"We need to know how many amps of power the band needs."

"I don't know. Give them a hundred amps."

"Are you crazy? You could run half the brothel on a hundred amps."

"Oh. Maybe I should call them."

"Good idea."

"Okay, I got it. They need thirty amps."

"How many tents do you have?"

"Eight tents, twenty-by-twenty each. We're also going to need power for the barbecue area and the bars."

"Where are you going to put the stage?"

"I think by the first villa."

"How big is it?"

"Well, that's another thing I think I might need your help with. You see, I don't have a stage. I thought maybe you could build one."

Neither James nor my husband was thrilled with me at that moment. It had to be a hundred and fifteen degrees outside and they were out there running power and now I needed them to build a stage. Both of them shot me a look. Okay, I'm going to my office now. They worked on the power until dark, but they got it done. I had the kitchen make them steak and lobster dinners. It was the least I could do.

"That wasn't too bad, was it?" I asked them. "So, when do you think you can start on the stage?"

Again with the look. Okay, I'll shut up now.

The following Saturday my husband and James built the stage.

"That looks great!"

"We still have to build the roof."

"It doesn't need a roof, the event is at night."

"We need something to mount the lights to."

"Oh, yeah."

This power stuff was really becoming a pain in the ass. By Sunday the stage was complete. Fernando painted it during the week. We got past that little setback and were back on track.

It was the final week before our event. I held a meeting with the staff so we could go over everything together. I passed out the schedule for Saturday listing everyone's hours and duties. The kitchen staff had been prepping all the food and the housekeepers had been scrubbing every inch of the building. Everything had to be perfect. Some departments would have double duty. Security would have to direct the vehicles for parking along with their security duties. The shift managers who were regularly scheduled to work would work their shifts, but the shift managers who would normally be off would work as hostesses, in the retail tent, or assist the bartenders.

"No one is to speak with the media or answer any questions they may have," I said. "All media, whether it is radio, TV or newspaper, are to be directed to me."

The brothel business, being as controversial as it was, could not afford any bad press. It was a standing rule at the brothel: No one talks to the media except the madam.

"No cameras or recording devices of any type are allowed. A sign will be posted by the brothel door stating that this is prohibited." After the meeting with the staff, it was time to meet with the ladies.

"Ladies, you will need to be absolutely stunning by six o'clock. The event will start at seven. At six o'clock please meet me in the dining room so that you can get your corsages." I ordered wristlet corsages for my ladies so they wouldn't be mistaken other ladies who may be attending the event.

"I know I don't have to tell you that I expect you to be on your best behavior. We will have a lot of VIPs here, so I don't want any arguing, no drama, and DON'T get drunk. With all the guests we are expecting, the bartenders will not be able to monitor your drinks, so you will be on the honor system. DO NOT GET DRUNK!"

We had a six-drink maximum in a twenty-four-hour period, from noon until noon, for the ladies. Whenever a lady ordered a drink from the bar, the bartender would have the lady sign for it. When she reached her sixth drink, she could not have any more until noon the next day. That policy was put in place for the ladies' personal safety. The lady must be in control of her party at all times. Should there be a problem, she needed to be coherent enough to press the panic button. There were panic buttons in each of the rooms, as well as in each of the special party rooms and villas. In addition, I didn't want a lady to be so drunk that her customer would take liberties he wasn't entitled to.

The safety of my ladies was always my primary concern. These ladies were in my custody when they were at the brothel and it was my responsibility to keep them safe. We never did have a problem with a customer during a party. The panic buttons were never used. We tested them every thirty days just to make sure they were working properly, just in case we ever needed them.

After our meeting, the ladies stopped by my office, one by one, to show me their outfits. For the most part, they chose to wear gowns, very sexy gowns. They looked like movie stars at the Academy Awards. They were beautiful.

I had some prepping of my own to do for our gala event. I needed a new outfit, new shoes, manicure, pedicure, and I had to get my hair done (my natural highlights were overtaking my head. I remember when they used to be blond; now they're gray!). With all the preparations for the event, I had almost forgotten about me. I took off early and headed to Las Vegas to do what I love best . . . shop!

I called on the way in and set up an appointment for a manicure, pedicure and, yes, my natural highlights. Thank God the salon I go to stayed open late during the summer. I hit the Fashion Show Mall on the Las Vegas Strip. I love that mall. It has everything I need, and then some. Nordstrom was screaming my name and I was there to answer the call. I headed toward the formal wear. I tried on gown after gown. I was looking for that one special gown, you know, the one that makes you look thin. I'll admit, I was asking a lot of that gown, but it had to be there. I always pictured myself thinner than I actually was — that is, until I looked in the mirror and, yup, there she was, the old, fat broad.

Finally, I found it. It was beautiful. A chocolate brown, satin gown draped with chocolate brown chiffon with gold bead work going from the right shoulder to the left hem line. The bead work wasn't overwhelming, it was just enough. Sometimes less is more. Stunning! I tried it on — not too bad. I grabbed the gown and headed to the shoe department. It didn't take as long to find the perfect shoes. I still had a few minutes before my salon appointment.

Now I could relax. Pedicure first, then manicure, and then those highlights. My hair is naturally dark brown. In my younger days my highlights were blond. Naturally, these days they are blond artificially. My hair style was similar to that of Liza Minnelli, except I have chunky, blond highlights. I love my hairdresser. In one hour she can shave ten years off my looks. Who wouldn't love someone like that?

I went home and my husband was already home from work. "I can't wait to show you my dress." No sooner did those words roll out of my mouth than I realized that I sounded just like the ladies!

Fernando, James, and my husband began setting up for the event four days before. Barbecues had to be placed, the stage was prepared, stairs were built for the stage, lights were strung on the cabanas by the pool, and tiki torches were strategically placed. We had done as much as we could for now.

Friday, the tents, the draft beer trailer, and the tables and chairs were delivered. Eight twenty-by-twenty tents were erected throughout the courtyard. Tables and chairs were set up all over, including rows in front of the stage. Everything was looking good!

I went to the kitchen to get some ice-cold energy drinks for the guys. It was so hot. It had to be one hundred and seventeen degrees outside.

That was the hottest July I could remember in a long time. I came out with a tray full of cold drinks. Where is everybody? There was no one to be found. I walked back into the brothel, looked all over, and couldn't find anyone. Their trucks were still there. As I was walking through the courtyard, I found them filing out of the draft trailer. Apparently it had been converted into a break room. They had lawn chairs set up in there and were kicking back, having a nice cold draft in an air-cooled trailer. Sure beat the hell out of my energy drinks!

Next, three bars were set up poolside. Up went the retail tent with two tables for our wares. The guys ran power to the tents, the stage, the barbecues, and the bars. It looked like clear sailing from here on out.

Clear sailing, my ass. It was Saturday, the day of our event. My husband and I were staying in our motorhome at the brothel. There had been so much work to do that it just wasn't feasible to drive back and forth from Las Vegas every day. I got up to go into the brothel for a cup of coffee and the wind was whipping around like crazy. All the tables and chairs were strewn across the courtyard. The tents looked like they were going to be airborne any minute.

Auntie Em! Auntie Em! This can't be happening! I sat on the step of the motorhome with tears streaming down my face. My husband came out and said, "Don't worry, the wind will die down. I'll call James, Ed, and Andrew (friends of ours) and they'll come out and help." Ed was coming out anyway because he was bringing a light tower from his work for the desert area we had graded to use for overflow parking.

The reinforcements arrived a couple of hours later. The wind was getting worse and black clouds were moving in. You've got to be kidding!

I called the entire security staff in and for the next three hours we all hung on to the tents. The wind was so strong it was lifting the tents right out of the ground. "If one of these lets loose, it's going to kill someone!" Andrew yelled. Andrew was a really nice guy — not very encouraging, but a real nice guy. With not much else to do but hang on for dear life, we were all laughing and joking. What the hell, you may as well have fun, right? We were out there for about an hour before the rain started.

The downpour lasted about forty minutes. Drenched and wind blown, we all just kept hanging on. And then, what was that? That bright spot in the sky. Could it be? It was. The sun started peeking through the clouds, and a short while later the wind stopped. Our arms were stiff and tired. I had such a death grip on my tent pole that when I finally let go, I couldn't lower my arms without wincing.

"Who wants a beer?" my husband asked as he made his way to the draft trailer. The hell with beer, I wanted a VO and water. Beer just wouldn't cut it, I needed whiskey. That VO and water sure tasted good.

It was one o'clock and we had to start all over. The tables and chairs had to be picked up, wiped off, and put back in place. The bars had to be stocked, the sodas, water, and bottled beer had to be iced down, the retail tent had to be stocked, the tablecloths and centerpieces had to be put on the tables. By the time this thing gets started, I'll be ready for a nap!

By five o'clock everything was done. The place looked great! The band arrived and started hooking up its equipment. I jumped in the shower and got ready.

At six o'clock I met all the ladies in the dining room. Each had a wristlet corsage to match her outfit. They looked absolutely stunning. Their hair was perfect, nails beautifully manicured, their make-up wouldn't have looked better if it were applied by a make-up artist. They looked like princesses.

"Remember, ladies, on your best behavior," I said sternly.

"Mom, you look so beautiful! Are you going to be in the line-up tonight, too?"

"Honey, there isn't a guy alive who can afford me. I charge by the pound," I joked. We were ready!

I peeked my head out the parlor door. There was a line of people as far as I could see. At seven o'clock, the parlor doors swung open and they came in.

My friend Ray was working the door for me. Ray was a tall, buff black man who had played professional football. The ladies took one look at him and they all offered to "do" him for free. Let's see, and the house gets half of that . . . no.

At eight o'clock people were still filing in. I looked around the courtyard and everyone seemed to be having a great time. The band was playing, people were dancing, eating, drinking, and laughing. It was a beautiful sight. The ladies were mingling with the crowd, and the brothel was busy, too. One after another, the ladies took eager gentlemen back to their rooms. I went to check on the shift manager and she was frantically booking parties. That, too, was a beautiful sight. I never would have have believed, when I was sitting on the steps of my motorhome that morning, that this night would turn out like it did.

I talked to everyone. I made sure I didn't overlook anyone. I approached one tent and it was full of the Red Hat ladies. There must have been eighty of them, all decked out in their purple and red outfits and those amazing red hats. I remember several guests asking me if they were former working girls. Hmmm, brothel alumni. No, they're just a group that would never miss a party!

I can't count the number of tours I gave that night. Everyone was so impressed by the brothel. But the villas were everyone's favorite. As the evening went on, I wasn't able to show the villas any longer as they were all in use. We even had parties waiting for the availability of the villas as soon as they were finished and cleaned. Can you believe it? It was like an airport with planes stacked awaiting take-off.

At three o'clock in the morning we started breaking down the bars and closed up the retail tent. Now the accounting process had to begin. There was so much money that I had piles of it strewn across the floor of my office. These piles were bar revenue, these piles were retail revenue, and these piles were from ticket sales. We had more than eleven hundred people here. Can you believe it? I guess I didn't have to worry about ruining my perfect record after all.

At four o'clock in the morning we still had quite a few guests. Everyone was having such a great time they didn't want to leave. Ed and Andrew crashed for the night in two of the ladies' rooms. The ladies wouldn't need them as they were in the villas for overnight parties. At five o'clock I decided I probably should go to bed and get some sleep. My husband was already sound asleep in the motorhome. I managed to sleep until about nine o'clock. I got up and trudged to the brothel for some breakfast. James was already in the dining room having tea. I got a cup of coffee and we sat and talked about the night before. Night before . . . hell, it was just a few hours ago!

No one was looking forward to cleaning up. A few minutes passed by and in came Fernando. "Good morning!" How can he be so spunky when it took everything in me to lift my coffee mug to my lips? Right behind Fernando was my husband. We ordered breakfast and planned the clean-up. As we were finishing our breakfast Ed walked in. It was more of a stagger than a walk, actually.

"Do you feel as bad as you look?" I asked. Ed was probably the nicest guy you would ever meet. I've known him for more than fifteen years and never seen him in a bad mood, not even when he was going through his divorce. His son and our son played football together. They started in Pop Warner when they were seven years old and played together all through high school.

"I'm pissed," Ed said. "I slept through four lineups and breakfast!"

You see, in the ladies' rooms was a bell system that we would ring when we had a lineup. When they were in a party in their rooms, there was a switch, like a light switch, that they would flip up and that would disengage the bell so they wouldn't be disturbed during a party. I guess

Ed didn't flip the switch.

We finished with cleaning up about noon. We all had lunch and then fled to our respective homes. We were beat. I couldn't have done it without the help of my husband and our friends.

Shortly after that first event, I received numerous phone calls asking if we were going to do it again next year. Why not? I received so many thank you notes from guests saying they never had such a good time as they did at the brothel. Even more perceptions changed.

Each year the event got bigger. It got so big that my friend Mack would fly in from New Jersey to help me out. Mack and I grew up together in New Jersey. He was the first friend I ever had. We've been friends since we were four years old. That was forty-seven years ago! Mack lived in the house behind mine. Did you ever have that one friend you could count on no matter what? For me, that was Mack. Some people don't experience that type of friendship during their entire lives. I am lucky to have a friend like Mack. He would fly in every year, at his own expense, just to help out with the event. I was always conscious of the bottom line, so any time I could get "free" help, I took it. We had the set-up down to an art. It became routine. Everyone knew their jobs; everyone knew how I wanted it to look. It ran like a finely tuned machine.

If wealth were measured by friendships, I mean real friendships, I would have to say that I am one of the richest women in the world. I have friends who would do anything for me, any time, anywhere, no questions asked. That's the kind of friends James, Andrew, Mack, and Ed were. Nothing was ever an imposition, nothing was ever a bother. But my best friend of all was my husband.

After our fourth annual event, they became bittersweet. Ed, who was there for every brothel function, came out to help with the event, just as he did all the years before. He towed the light tower out, just as he did all the years before. That year, though, he didn't stay the night at the brothel. He had to take his youngest son to football camp early the next morning, so he drove home that night. Ed never made it home. He was killed in a crash seventeen miles from his home. After that, the event was never quite the same. I'll never forget the day Ed died.

Chapter Eleven

The Expansion

Things at the brothel were going well, so well that the owners decided to expand. Why not? You can't have too much of a good thing, right? Then it's settled. We'll build a hotel and a full-service spa. No "happy endings" in this spa, though. You'd have to go over to the brothel for that. Meetings were held, plans were drawn, and before you knew it, we were moving dirt. There wouldn't be another brothel like this anywhere in the world.

Fernando's maintenance shop was demolished. We'd build him a new one. Poor Fernando, he had to work out of a forty-foot storage container throughout the hot summer.

Construction started slowly. If there was a line buried underground, the construction crew found it and broke it. They broke water lines, power lines, even the gas line. This was more like destruction than construction. Every time I turned around, construction came to a screeching halt due to some sort of broken line. The fire line was the worst. I remember the construction foreman coming into the brothel, yelling for me.

"Madam, we have a slight problem."

"You couldn't have broken another line, you broke them all already."

"No, ma'am, there was one we missed, but we got it today . . . the fire line. It seems we flooded quite a few acres."

The fire line, a water line that fed the brothel's fire system, was an eighteen-inch steel pipe.

"How the hell could you break the fire line?"

"We were digging with the backhoe, ma'am." He almost sounded proud of himself, as if it was quite an accomplishment to break the fire line. I was ready to kill him!

I followed the foreman out to the construction site. I went traipsing through muck in my Nordstrom shoes. Are you kidding me? Now I'm really pissed. Forget the fire line, what about my shoes?

It took weeks for the area to dry out. When we started up construction again, here came the monsoons. A week of rain, just what we needed. It took another week to dry things out and we were ready to start again.

Things started looking up. The framing was done; it was beginning to look like something now. The weather was working in our favor; it appeared the worst was over. Sure, maybe for someone else, but not for me!

The housing market was booming in Las Vegas. People were bidding against one another to buy homes. Homes were selling for far more than they were worth. The builders jumped on the bandwagon and construction in Las Vegas was everywhere. It didn't matter what part of town you were in, they were building. The federal Bureau of Land Management was auctioning off thousands of acres of public land on the edges of Las Vegas and developers were buying them up as soon as they became available. The price of building supplies skyrocketed. Everyone was making tons of money and people were still coming to Las Vegas in droves. Real estate agents were making a fortune. Houses wouldn't be on the market for more than a day before they were snapped up. It was crazy.

I suppose my contractor felt left out. He walked off the job and went to Las Vegas to find his fortune. It was like the gold rush all over again. Now what? I couldn't get another contractor, because they were all in Las Vegas chasing their fortunes. Believe me, it wasn't for lack of trying either. I called them all. The conversations were more or less the same.

"Hello, I need a contractor to finish a commercial job for me."

"We may be able to help you. Where is this job?"

"In Pahrump."

"Lady, you can't be serious." Click.

I am the type of person for whom "no" is not an option. So, I temporarily tucked my elaborate wardrobe away and pulled out my jeans, T-shirts, and sneakers. I had a plan. I'll hire local tradesmen in Pahrump to do the work and I'll oversee them. How hard could it be? The framing was already done. How much more could there be? Walls, plumbing, power (again with the power), floors, a roof? It couldn't be that difficult. That was my plan.

All summer, Fernando and I were out on the construction site. We started early in the morning and worked until the sun set. I was picking out tile, carpeting, blinds, and all the stuff for the spa. I ordered a Jacuzzi tub and a sauna kit online. One Sunday morning while having coffee with my husband, I finally got up the nerve to ask the question.

"How would you like to build a sauna for me?"

"Are you crazy? I don't know how to build a sauna."

"Well, it's wood. You work with wood all day, it shouldn't be too hard."

"I build custom picture frames!"

"Come on, I have all the stuff and the plans. It's like an erector set. It will be fun. I'll help you."

He agreed on one condition — that I wouldn't help.

"Okay, fine."

The following week, my husband came out to the brothel and started building my sauna. There actually was quite a bit more involved, as I forgot about the benches, the light, the heater and, you guessed it, the POWER. The poor guy was working on this thing for about two weeks in the hottest part of the summer. I can't believe he is still married to me.

When the sauna was finished, it looked great. What a fantastic job. You would have never believed he didn't build these things for a living.

The Jacuzzi went in pretty smoothly. The steam room made up for the ease of building the Jacuzzi. The steam room was a bitch. I couldn't find anyone in Pahrump who knew how to plumb a steam room. I had bought a steam generator online (you gotta love the Internet) and it came with directions, so what's the problem? There wasn't anyone I could find who wanted to take on this steam room. I called the company I bought the steam generator from and talked to a guy named Wade. I told Wade my tale of woe.

"Where is this place?"

"It's in Pahrump, Nevada."

"Isn't that where those prostitution houses are?"

"Well, actually, we are one of those prostitution houses. We're building a spa here at the brothel and I really need your help."

Once Wade heard we were a "prostitution house," he suddenly became more eager to help me.

"I'll tell you what I can do. I can fly out there and get you all hooked up. You'll have to buy some tools, though. I can't take them with me, not since 9/11."

"Not a problem. Just let me know what you need and we'll have them for you."

The following week Wade showed up. He was like a kid in a candy store. When he walked in and saw the ladies wearing next to nothing, I thought his eyes were going to pop out of his head.

"Hello, Wade, I'm the madam. We spoke on the phone."

"You sure don't see nothing like this in Nebraska. Can I take some pictures?"

"I would prefer that you didn't, but I can get you one of our menus signed by all the ladies. Would you like that?"

"Yes, ma'am, I sure would."

Wade did what he promised. He got the steam room up and running. And I did what I promised. I got him a menu signed by all the ladies.

When I started at the brothel, it had a menu. It was a two-page pamphlet photocopied on colored paper. Shortly after the new brothel was completed, I got to work on a new menu. The new menu was more of a magazine actually. It was fifty-four pages, a complete pictorial of the brothel and the ladies and, of course, the menu items took center stage.

As you can imagine, our menu was a bit different from your typical restaurant menu. "Appetizers" consisted of foreplay activities. "Entrees" were your main courses consisting of a variety of sexual activities. Menu items, such as a Parisian Frappe, were certainly a lot different from any frappe you would order at Starbucks. Our frappe was oral sex on the rocks! The lady would have ice in her mouth while performing orally on her customer. Half 'n' Half was no longer something you put in your coffee, but rather a combination of oral sex and intercourse. Suds and Bubbles was an aquatic sexual experience involving being submersed, from the neck down, in a provocatively deep Jacuzzi jetted tub. The Slip and Slide was not for kids! It was an adult playground consisting of sensual oils and flesh. All the menu items were explained in great detail so there was no doubt as to what your encounter would consist of. Not only was it entertaining, it was educational. People would come in just to buy the magazine and try some of the menu items at home. I designed a sexy cover that compelled you to pick up the magazine. Full color, glossy finish. It was a work of art!

"Wow, when you said a menu, I wasn't expecting anything like this!" Wade was reading through the menu like he was studying for the bar exam. "What is this here, this 'Hot and Cold French'?"

"That is an oral technique," I explained, "where the lady puts liquids of different temperatures in her mouth and then performs orally on you."

"What about this one, 'S&M'?"

"That is a dominance party which takes place in our dungeon."

"You have a dungeon?"

"Would you like to see it?"

I showed Wade to the dungeon and there were those wide eyes again. "I can't believe it. I've heard about these kinds of things, but I never thought I would ever see one." Wade was enchanted by the throne in the corner of the S&M dungeon. "What's that chair for?" he asked.

"That is a throne where the mistress sits and chains her subject at her feet where they are readily available to receive her wrath."

The throne was custom built for us by Michael, a friend of James. He built a huge throne all decked out in black leather and silver studs. Chains and shackles were mounted on the oversized wooden arm rests. The throne was placed on a ten-inch platform. Michael built the throne for us in his garage at his home in Las Vegas. While he was working on it, before it was painted black, the neighborhood kids asked if he was building a chair for Santa. "Not exactly," Michael answered.

"Well, I have your bill here for my work," Wade said, "but do you think we could maybe work something out?"

"Do you mean in trade? I'm sure we could work something out."

I took a look at Wade's bill and I was grateful he wanted to take it out in trade. Between the airfare, parts and labor, I was ahead of the game at fifty cents on the dollar. The house was getting its half in trade and would have to pay the lady her half.

"Did you see anyone in particular you might like to speak with or would you prefer to have a lineup?"

"Oh, no, ma'am, I had my eye on that cute little blonde in that bright pink negligee."

"That's Candace. I'll get her for you. Just have a seat here and I'll be right back."

It seemed Wade was really intrigued by the dungeon and quite the adventurous type. Who would have thought? Candace was very experienced in dominance parties and it was certain that she would give Wade something to remember long after he left the brothel. After his party, I showed Wade to the door. He didn't look me in the eye after his party, but his smile said it all. "We hope to see you again, Wade."

"Oh, well, thank you, madam. I think you will. Yes, I think you will."

The spa was coming together nicely. The Jacuzzi was done, the sauna was done, the steam room was done (and so was Wade). All that needed to be completed now was the reception area and the furnishings.

I had been buying furniture for the spa and the hotel rooms. The hotel suites would be themed, like the villas, and the standard rooms would be furnished identically. I had my heart set on decorating one of the suites in a pirate theme. Do you think I could find any furniture that looked even remotely pirate-ish? Of course not. Well, you always need a back-up plan and I had mine: my husband. He could build pirate furniture for me! I asked him how he felt about building the furniture for the pirate suite and to my surprise he didn't pitch a fit. (After the sauna, I was a little gun-shy.)

He burnt all the wood to give it an aged look, and built all the countertops, the mantle over the fireplace, the coffee tables, night stands, armoire, everything. He even built a ship mast, with sails and a parrot in the crow's nest. It looked great. While he was moving everything in, I was decorating. I bought mooring ropes, fishing nets, pirate figurines, a pirate hat, old rum bottles, and anything and everything you could imagine. The suite was ready for Mr. Bones to move in. Mr. Bones was a skeleton sitting by and guarding his treasure chest spilling over with gold coins and jewels. What kind of pirate suite wouldn't have a treasure chest?

Yes, it was all coming together. Fernando's new maintenance shop was completed and he was so happy to move out of his storage trailer. Although Fernando never complained, I knew he was glad to have an air-conditioned shop again.

The time came around quickly for our annual event and we were going to showcase our expansion. Yes, we'd include the hotel and spa in the tour. The event was right around the corner and the furniture wasn't moved into the rooms. The countertops for the bathrooms were all cut to the wrong size and the new ones weren't here yet. I don't care. Move the furniture in anyway. The Wednesday before the event, the countertops came in and were installed. The guys were there to install the mirrors in the bathrooms, too. Wait, why are they taking the mirrors back to their truck? They're the wrong size, too? You've got to be kidding me. I never thought of a tape measure as being a difficult tool to use or comprehend. Why are we having these problems? I ran over to the truck and flagged down the mirror guy.

"I have to have these cut to the right size and installed no later than Friday."

"We'll try our best."

"Trying your best isn't good enough. I have to have them Friday."

"Friday, I don't think that would be possible."

"If you get these done and installed by Friday, I'll put you and your crew on the VIP list for our annual event on Saturday."

"It'll be done. Thank you, madam."

Every problem has a solution.

I was going crazy trying to get the hotel furnished and stocked and setting up for the event at the same time. The usual suspects were back to help: my husband, James, Andrew, and Mack. At least they could stay in the hotel this year. That is, if I get it finished!

Thursday morning we have our fire inspection and, I hope, receive the certificate of occupancy. Fernando and I are doing the walk-through with the fire marshal. He wants more sprinklers. But what we have is what the plans called for. How can he say he wants more sprinklers? Because he's the fire marshal, that's why.

"I promise we will put in all the additional sprinklers you want, sir, but you know we are having our annual event on Saturday and I really need these rooms."

"I'll give you a temporary certificate of occupancy, but I want these sprinklers in no later than two weeks," he says.

"It will be done. Thank you."

Finally, I catch a break!

I was a reservations manager in a Las Vegas hotel-casino before I was an executive host, so the reservations system was a breeze, at least to me. The shift managers, who would be working with the system, were another story, however. We have only twelve rooms, so it shouldn't have been that difficult. But it was a nightmare. They checked people in to dirty rooms; they checked people in to occupied rooms. You name it, they did it. This wasn't the Bellagio. How hard could it be to keep track of twelve rooms?

I kept fine tuning the system. I put "Dirty Room Logs" into place, even though there was a built-in system in the reservations program, I had security check all the vacant rooms to make sure they were clean, I did anything and everything to make sure we didn't look like idiots to our guests. It was only twelve rooms!

Andrew, I think, was the happiest to stay in the hotel. In previous years he had stayed in one of the brothel rooms and we would torment him throughout the night. There was a monitoring system in all the ladies' rooms. All negotiations were monitored by a two-way speaker installed in the ceiling. When Andrew would stay in one of those rooms, we would wait until he fell asleep. (It was easy to tell when he was asleep as Andrew snored loudly.) Then we would call to him through the speaker. Andrew never did figure out where that voice came from. He would get up the following morning and when I would ask him how he slept, he'd say, "I kept waking up. I thought I heard someone calling my name, but no one was there. I must have been dreaming." It was cheap entertainment for us, even though it was at Andrew's expense. After he spent the night in the hotel, Andrew said he slept like a baby.

The landscapers were planting trees, shrubs, and flowers, and laying sod. They still had so much to do and the event was tomorrow. The tents, tables, and chairs were delivered and everyone was falling over everyone else trying to get things done. The landscapers were upset because people kept walking through with tables and chairs. They were really upset when a big truck full of tents pulled in. By sunset on Friday, they still weren't done. We were, but they weren't.

Saturday morning the landscapers were back. "You have to finish by three o'clock," I told one of the guys. He just looked at me and grinned. He didn't speak English. Where's Fernando? Fernando told him, in Spanish, that they needed to be done by three o'clock. They finished at four-thirty. Talk about cutting it close!

It was another successful event. Everyone seemed to love the hotel and spa. With each event, I got a little smarter. I walked all night long, mingling, schmoozing, and conducting tours, those endless tours. Now, the tour was even bigger. I brought slippers with me that year, fancy slippers that I would put on after a few hours. By that time, who would notice? Most everybody would be drunk by then anyway. Oh yeah, much better.

A short time after the hotel opened, we put in tennis courts, flower gardens, and a huge water feature in the center of the garden. The place was amazing.

Chapter Twelve

CHANGING PERCEPTIONS

We were making history. The brothel industry had come a long way from those small, dark, dingy trailers. Other brothels were following in our footsteps. They started building stick-built structures; no more trailers. Villas were springing up at other brothels. None was as lavish as ours, but the industry as a whole was taking a step up. Those steps made it better for working girls throughout the industry.

Years ago, the working girls were treated very poorly. They were not only sexually abused by brothel owners, but verbally abused as well. They didn't have a voice and their opinions were to be kept to themselves. What we did really helped to change things for them. We catered to our ladies. I pampered them, cared for them, but most important, I listened to them. They are no different from the rest of us. They have thoughts and feelings just like everyone else. So, why had they been treated differently? That was something I could never understand and certainly would never condone.

I can remember, on more than one occasion, coming to work and finding a working girl curled up asleep on the front steps of the brothel, using her coat as a blanket. It seems she had refused to have sex with the owner of the brothel she was working for, so he took her money and threw her out in the middle of the night. It usually was the younger girls who refused. The ones who had been in the business for a while were accustomed to this practice and, although they didn't want to, felt forced to oblige. The young girls would walk alone in the desert at night until they reached the doorstep of my brothel. What is wrong with some people? I would take them in and show them the more humane side of the industry. You see, perceptions needed to change even among the working girls.

There are some brothels today that still operate under the old thought processes, but others mirror our practices. It is true: Imitation is the best form of flattery.

In the case of our brothel, a new company with a new way of thinking changed things for the most part. I remember when I started. I was told by everyone in the business that I would never make it because I was not a former working girl. Every madam had been a former working girl, I was told. But I was used to being the underdog, so I believed I would do just fine. And I did. I never gave a tour when someone didn't ask, "Were you in the business before?"

"No," I'd reply, "I'm not a former working girl."

The next question was always the same. "Then how did you get into this business?"

"I'm not sure, perhaps a weak moment."

Oh, we were definitely a trendsetter. All the things that people said couldn't be done, we did — and we did them well. There were no brothels that held the events that we did. They did not have a hotel, or a spa, or tennis courts. We were considered a "respectable" place by most. There were still those who looked down their noses, but I just kept at it, changing perceptions one at a time.

I remember when I received a call from Mensa. The group was holding a convention at a hotel in Las Vegas and asked if I would speak. Mensa, imagine that? This is an organization of smart people, and they want to hear me speak? Public speaking about legal prostitution? Sure, why not.

A week before the convention, I received another phone call from the group. "Madam, we're going to have to move you to another hall."

"Why, are not enough people going to show?"

"On the contrary, so many members have signed up to hear you speak that we need to move you to a larger hall. We have never had so many people sign up to hear a speaker before."

My husband drove me to the hotel and on the way there he asked if I had my speech ready.

"No, I didn't prepare one. I'll just ad-lib." To be honest, I didn't even think of preparing a speech. I figured I would speak just as I live my life. Sometimes things just work out better that way.

The hall was packed. There must have been two thousand people. I was introduced at the podium and away I went. I spoke for fifteen to twenty minutes about the brothel industry and then I opened it up for questions. They had so many great questions. Of course they did, they're Mensa; they're smart! I always felt that it was better to speak less and let people ask questions. That way, you know you are giving them the information they want. It's the whole less-is-more thing. I was up on the podium for two and a half hours answering questions. They were so curious. I summed it all up by telling them that it didn't matter to me if they were for legal prostitution or against it, but it was always my goal that people wouldn't be so naive to believe that if there wasn't legal prostitution, there wouldn't be prostitution. Prostitution is everywhere, so why not control it and keep it clean and safe? That's my philosophy.

Afterward, they came up to the podium, shook my hand, and thanked me for enlightening them. "You speak with such passion," many of them said. I do. Passion is a byproduct of something you truly believe in.

They expressed so much interest and wanted to see the brothel, so I arranged a tour for them. The following day two busloads of Mensa members pulled up to the brothel. I broke them into smaller groups so they could see and hear everything. We held tour after tour until everyone had gone through the brothel. They were in awe. They couldn't believe what they saw.

"This place is immaculate!"

"I had no idea that it would be this nice."

"What an unbelievable place you have here."

"You have made quite an impact on us."

"I have quite a different outlook on prostitution now."

"And the ladies, well, they're all gorgeous and friendly too!"

The comments went on and on.

Imagine that, a madam impressing Mensa. Can you believe it? They certainly were smart!

Yet even more perceptions changed.

I found myself speaking at colleges and other venues. The topic? Legal prostitution vs. illegal prostitution. One definition of the word "prostitute" is "one who sells one's abilities, talent, or name for an unworthy purpose." If we are being totally honest, we've all prostituted ourselves at one point or another. Whether it was for our beauty, brawn, or brains, we've all done it. If you have ever worked for someone other than yourself, you have sold your ability or talent. After all, that's what landed you the job in the first place. I guess the only real argument is whether you believe the purpose to be "worthy" or "unworthy." We have all worked for our self-benefit. Is that worthy or unworthy? "Worthy" is defined as "having worth, merit or value." Therefore, I believe the argument lies with the word "unworthy."

Oh, there are those who will condemn prostitution and anyone who may be associated with it. I can remember many battles with "crusaders" who were determined to close down the brothels. Most of the church groups were on this mission. I have nothing against churches of any kind. I was raised Catholic myself. I went to church when I was growing up. I believe in God. I pray. I obey the Ten Commandments. But I don't pass judgment on anyone, regardless of their chosen career path. That's not my job. I'll leave that up to sources much higher than myself.

The brothel was legal! We had a business license. We paid taxes to the state. We came to the aid of the town when it needed emergency equipment for its police and fire departments. We bought them their ambulance. We didn't pass a bill or propose a bond issue to raise anyone's taxes to pay for these things, as our politicians do. They needed help, and we helped.

I once received a letter from a very grateful man who was transported to a hospital in Las Vegas by the ambulance we purchased for the town. Pahrump didn't have a hospital of its own at that time, so people had to be transported sixty miles away to a hospital in Las Vegas. This man had suffered a heart attack, and on the ride to Las Vegas the paramedic told him that the brothel had bought the town this ambulance. The man pulled through. When he was released and returned to his home in Pahrump, he wrote the brothel a letter of thanks for purchasing the ambulance. "You and your wonderful ladies saved my life. I will be forever grateful" he wrote. I suppose he was right. In a sense, we did help save his life. Yet another perception changed.

The brothel chose to fly under the radar. We did not publicize what we monetarily contributed to. It was better that way. But the local people knew. Somehow word would get out. We put in baseball diamonds, soccer fields, and all sorts of things. The kids didn't need to know where the money for these things came from, they just needed the baseball diamonds and soccer fields.

Yet, when many people think of brothels, they think of dirty, little trailers at the end of a long, lonely road. Well, not this one. We've given them some things to really think about. Think about the safe haven we've created for the ladies who work in this profession. Think about the safe haven we've created for the customers who choose to use their services.

Prostitution runs rampant in Las Vegas. It's illegal, but that doesn't mean it doesn't exist. How many crimes have gone unreported because of illegal prostitution? You can't call the police after you've been robbed in your Las Vegas hotel room by a prostitute. You've broken the law yourself by soliciting the services of a prostitute. And what about extortion? It's not uncommon for an illegal prostitute to drug her client, take photos of him in some very compromising situations and then extort money from him once he's regained consciousness. You wouldn't want your wife to see those photos, would you? Hell, you could lose everything . . . your wife, your kids, your job, everything you've worked so hard for.

The ladies who worked at the brothel had sheriff's cards, they underwent background checks, they were fingerprinted. They weren't criminals. If they were, they couldn't get a sheriff's card. We took precautions, just like any legal entity. When people think of brothels, they think of sex for money. It's true; they do sell sex for money. But what the customer is really paying for is the safety and security that comes along with that sex. How could you put a price tag on your safety, security, and well being?

Hand in hand with illegal prostitution ultimately comes disease. Illegal prostitutes aren't tested for STDs or HIV. Hell, most of them don't even use condoms. Oh yeah, you could get lucky and pick up an illegal prostitute and not get robbed or beaten by her pimp, but what about disease? Do you know for a fact that she is "clean"? The ladies at the brothel were tested for STDs and HIV every time they arrived at the brothel. It didn't matter if they just left two days ago. Every time they arrived, they were tested. They aren't allowed to "work the floor" until the brothel receives written confirmation from the lab that they, in fact, are free of STDs and HIV.

And condoms? They're mandatory. It's the law. There are Nevada Revised Statutes that govern the brothels. It isn't up for debate. Oh sure, there are customers who would offer the ladies more money to service them without a condom. The ladies never would. They wouldn't put their lives and careers at stake for a few extra dollars. They wouldn't risk jeopardizing hundreds of thousands of dollars to merely make a few hundred or even a thousand dollars extra. Would you? Of course not. They made a lot of money doing what they did. At the brothel, you never left with anything other than what you came in with. The only parting gifts you left with from the brothel were the ones you bought in the gift shop!

These were some of the things I found myself speaking about to different organizations that would call on me. Oh yes, we gave them a lot to think about.

Chapter Thirteen

HITTING THE ROAD

As with any other legal business, getting your name out to the public was a priority of the brothel. But at that time, state statutes prohibited us from advertising. As a result, the website was our best marketing tool. The website wasn't thought of as "advertising," as it was owned by the company and existed for "informational" purposes only.

I tracked everything. I spoke with everyone who came to the brothel when I was on the property. I wanted to know how customers learned about our existence. About eighty percent of them found us through our website.

What about the other twenty percent? If they couldn't find us, I felt compelled to find them. Maybe, I thought, there are some kind of "trade shows." Are you kidding me? Trade shows for sex? Oh, this job must really be taking its toll on me. What the hell could I have been thinking?

Well, I came to learn that there are trade shows for everything. After doing some research, I signed up to be an "exhibitor" at an erotica show in Los Angeles. Of course L.A. would have something like that; it has everything.

Naturally I solicited (more like coerced) my husband into going with me. I'm not going to a sex show by myself. What am I, nuts? It was a three-day show. I thought it might be a good idea to take one of the ladies with me to help work the booth and for people to see what type of ladies they could expect to spend some quality time with at the brothel.

This was not one of my better ideas.

We packed up and drove to Los Angeles. We checked in to our hotel and headed over to the convention center. In our booth at the convention, we had a video tour of the brothel playing on a VCR, brochures, menus, maps — you know, all the printed collateral a business would employ to display its wares. The booth was decked out in large, full-color photos of some of the ladies of the brothel.

It was a pretty big convention and I was amazed at some of the things I saw. There were vendors that sold life-like sex dolls. They cost thousands of dollars and people were lined up to place their orders. Each doll was built to the buyer's specifications. You could get blondes, brunettes, redheads, long hair, short hair, African-American dolls, Caucasian dolls, Asian dolls, whatever you wanted. I realized they were selling "manufactured" lineups. I had all of that, except mine were real, live, breathing sex dolls who actually had orgasms. Bet their dolls couldn't do that!

There were vendors who sold all kinds of enhancement devices for all types of sexual activities, including pills, oils, lotions, pumps for penises, pumps for breasts. Who thinks of these things?

One vendor stopped by my booth to give me his card. "Our booth is right down the aisle from you. You should stop by. I think we have some things you may be interested in for your brothel." Sure, why not. I took a walk to his booth. He sold furniture. Oh, no, not your typical furniture. You wouldn't see anything like this at Ethan Allen. No, he had a special line . . . sex furniture. You need special furniture to have sex?

"Oh, hi, I'm glad you found time to visit. Let me show you how this works. You see, this furniture contours your body to the perfect angle so that no matter what, your "g-spot" is in perfect alignment for orgasm after orgasm." Again, I have to ask: Who thinks of these things? I didn't buy any of his furniture.

The first day of the show just flew by. Our booth interested most of the passers-by. Our lady answered question after question and invited everyone to the brothel to visit her. Everybody had the same question: "How much does it cost?" It was a question that couldn't be answered for two reasons. First of all, the ladies were independent contractors who negotiated their own prices. Second was the fact that if she did quote a price, she could be arrested for soliciting. All the ladies were very well aware of that and never quoted any prices.

This particular lady, Dolce, was very pretty and a good choice to bring to the convention. At least that's what I thought at the time. After the first day of the convention ended we went back to our hotel. We had dinner, a couple of drinks, and went to our rooms. "We have another full day tomorrow, so let's get our rest," I said.

I was up all night. It seemed that Dolce was very enterprising, and so when an opportunity presented itself, she took advantage of it. Remember all those people she spoke with at the convention and invited to visit her at the brothel? As it turned out, she had invited them to her hotel room! About three o'clock in the morning there was a knock on my door.

"Mom, hurry up, open the door."

I went to the door and there was Dolce, standing in the hallway in her see-through negligee, holding it up in front of her, like a tray, and on it was a huge pile of cash.

"What the hell is that?"

"I've been busy, Mom. While you were sleeping, I was working."

"Working? Are you crazy? It's against the law here. You'll get us all arrested."

I whisked her in the room. "You're going back to your room and you're going to SLEEP."

I went back to my room, but I stood by my door listening and within five minutes I heard her door open.

"Oh, no you don't, you're done for the night. You're done for tomorrow night too."

I put her back in her room and stood guard by her door for the remainder of the night. Never again. The next night, in pursuit of sleep, my husband slept in her room and I kept her in my room with me. Kids, you gotta love 'em.

Finally the show came to an end and we headed home. I gave Dolce her money; after all, she earned it. That was the last time I ever took a lady out of town for anything.

The Adult Video News Convention, or AVN, is held in Las Vegas every year. This is a convention for adult videos. It is attended by tens of thousands of people. It ran for four days, but at least I could go home every night. So, the brothel reserved a space and off we went to AVN.

The first time we were an "exhibitor" at AVN, I remember walking through it in total amazement. There was every adult film company imaginable there. Everywhere you looked there were enormous screens playing the latest porn movies. Oh yeah, this is just what I need. I don't get enough of this at work. You've got to be kidding me. Along with the video was the audio, right? Of course, not only do they want you to see it, you have to hear it, too. Great. Don't get me wrong. I'm not a prude or anything, but if I am going to watch porn, it wouldn't be with twenty thousand people I don't even know!

What has my life become? I remember going to gaming conventions. I'd check out the new slot games, table games, computerized player tracking systems — you know, all the latest and greatest in the world of gaming. Now this. I've become the Queen of Porn!

When I would take a break from working the booth, I would wander through the convention and shop. I bought updated equipment for the S&M dungeon. I remember walking into one booth and they must have thought Rockefeller had just walked in. I was buying everything. "I'll take one of those spanking benches, some of those paddles, some of those collars and chains, those restraints, some of these, some of those . . ." The guy looked at me like he'd just hit the lottery.

I bought several pieces of furniture for the Dungeon. How was I going to get that stuff out of there? I called my son and asked him to meet me after the convention was over and put everything in his truck. He looked at me like I was crazy.

"What is all that stuff? I don't even want it in my truck!" he said.

"Just take it home and I'll take it to the brothel tomorrow," I answered.

I put everything in my living room until I went to work the next day. My son went out on a date that night, so of course while he was gone my husband and I set up all the stuff in his room. I knew he would bring the girl home after we had gone to sleep. She took one look at all that S&M paraphernalia and I don't believe my son ever saw her again. If you can't torment your kids every now and then, where's the fun?

As it turned out, the AVN Convention proved to be very lucrative for the brothel. The attendees came to Las Vegas from all over the world to see this. When they found out that there was a legal brothel only about an hour away, they were ecstatic.

We did AVN every year. Each year our booth was better and better. We eventually ran a shuttle between the convention and the brothel.

Year after year I saw many of the same vendors at the convention. That's how one of the major porn production companies came to shoot its next movie at the brothel.

A lot of porn stars came to AVN and they would hold autograph sessions. You should have seen the lines. People were lined up around the convention center waiting to get autographs from their favorite porn stars. One of the stars who produced her own movies came up to me and asked if I would be interested in letting them shoot their next movie at the brothel. "We would put the name of your brothel on the cover of the movie," I was informed. This was one of the biggest names in the porn industry. Sure, why not? We'd never done anything like that before.

A month or so later, the cast and film crew showed up at the brothel to shoot. They did most of the filming in one of the villas. Now, if you've never seen porn filmed before, I'm here to tell you, there isn't anything to compare it with. It was bizarre. The sex is real and they have "fluffers." Fluffers are wannabe porn stars whose job consists of keeping the male star hard between scenes. Can you imagine? I thought my job was unusual. They would be in the middle of a sex scene, going at it hot and heavy, and then all of a sudden, "Cut!" They would stop, make some adjustments, and pick up right where they left off. It was insane! They filmed for about two days and afterward we had a wrap party for them in the bar.

They had a blast filming at the brothel, getting to know the ladies and the staff. It was something everyone talked about for quite some time. Nothing like filming a porn movie to break up the day-to-day monotony!

I was working in my office one day when my phone rang. "Yes, this is the madam."

"Your presence is requested at our awards banquet, as your brothel has been nominated for an award." Awards banquet? What award, who nominated us, and who votes on something like this? Is there some sort of brothel academy out there?

I came to learn that there is quite a large group of "posters" on the Internet who had formed some type of cyber-awards competition for the brothels throughout the state of Nevada. They would post reviews about their experiences at brothels, post reviews of the ladies they partied with, and post reviews on the customer service they received. These "posters," as they were referred to by the ladies, were really big advocates for legalized prostitution. They were, for the most part, a great group of guys. They kind of watched over the Internet bulletin boards and protected the ladies. As with any group, there was a jerk or two among them, and those were the ones they would keep in check on the Internet. If someone posted something not so nice about any lady, these guys were tapping away at their keyboards in a split second to come to the lady's defense.

They would visit the brothels and, like the ladies, they would use another name to protect their identities. Over the years I came to know quite a number of posters and I consider them friends. I am still in touch with some of them today.

The posters have annual, sometimes twice-annual gatherings and hold them at different brothels. We would prepare a buffet for them. They always had the best time at our brothel. Not only did they party, but they would stay at the hotel and hang out in the bar. We just had a ball! They were some of the nicest people you'd ever want to meet and had great senses of humor. We were always sorry to see them leave, but it was consoling to know they would soon be back.

One time we conducted a "reverse lineup" for them. Instead of having the ladies line up, we had the posters do so. The ladies sat on the couch and picked their man. They got such a kick out if it. We all did. And the posters really knew how to strut their stuff. It was hysterical.

Okay, back to the awards banquet. The posters nominated different people for different awards, then they would vote and hold an awards banquet in Northern Nevada. There were many different categories, including "brothel of the year," "most improved brothel," and "best courtesan of the year." Our brothel was nominated for the "most improved brothel" award.

Oh yeah, my husband was going with me again. I'm not going by myself. This poor guy, what I put him through, he should get an award!

I couldn't imagine what one could possibly wear to a brothel awards banquet. There would be other madams there, so I've got to stand out. My brothel is up for an award and I am its representative. What pressure! I'm sure I can concoct some sort of outfit. Who knows, we might win! I might have to go up to the podium and accept the award on behalf of the brothel. "I'd like to thank the academy . . ."

My husband and I flew up to Northern Nevada. Every night there was a different party at a different brothel. The whole bit, with red carpet. Of course there was red carpet, we're brothels! The posters took this stuff seriously.

Now, remember when I said everyone has preconceived notions of what brothels look like — dark, dirty trailers at the end of a long, lonely road? Unfortunately, what I saw after visiting other brothels more or less confirmed those notions. I felt like I had gone back in time to my brothel! My head was flooded with memories of how my brothel used to look, the darkness, the dirt, the filth.

Our first stop was this little cul-de-sac where four or five brothels were clustered. They were hosting parties the night before the awards banquet. Now, you know we didn't catch them by surprise. We were invited, so don't you think they would have cleaned up the place, even a little bit? Was I the only one in the business who thought that way? Apparently, so.

The night of the awards banquet, I got dolled up in black-sequined gown, jewels dripping from my neck, ears, arms, and hands. I wore a black hat with a big brim, slightly cocked to one side. I definitely would be noticed. I definitely would stand out, and what a fine representative for my brothel. Oh my, I looked darling!

Most everyone in the industry was there. The nominated courtesans, referred to by the Internet posters as LPINs (Licensed Prostitutes in Nevada), were all there, as well as madams, brothel owners, posters, and others. We had dinner and then the ceremony began.

"And the winner of the most improved brothel is. . . ."

It was us!

"Accepting this award on behalf of the brothel is madam . . ."

That's me! I walked up to the podium. The people stood and clapped as I passed. They were shaking my hand and hugging me as I made my way up to the podium. I felt like I had just won an Oscar.

"Thank you, everyone, for your nomination and your votes. You know, when I began in this business, the industry had me doomed before I even got started. As I look out over the crowd tonight, I am happy to say that my friends are among the crowd. Our brothel has started something in this industry. Let's face it, in this business there aren't a lot of 'firsts' for anyone. But all of us are changing all of that. Our brothel was the first to have a madam who wasn't a former working girl, although I must say, in this get-up, I think I could make some money tonight! Our brothel was the first to put up a marquee sign. Our brothel was the first to take down the fence and let people walk right in, instead of being "buzzed" in through a locked gate. Our brothel was the first to welcome single women. Our brothel was the first to provide an atmosphere that pampers the customers AND the ladies; and our brothel was the first to become an adult destination resort. Your support of these concepts has helped make it all possible and for that I thank each and every one of you."

As I left the podium and looked over the crowd, they were all on their feet. A standing ovation! Can you believe it? I was clutching my award and held it tight to my chest, like I was some kind of running back and the entire defense was chasing me.

The crystal, octagon-shaped award read, "Most Improved Brothel of the Year." It was in a blue velvet-lined box and would be proudly displayed in the china closet in our parlor.

After the ceremony, everyone mingled over cocktails. I talked to many people in the industry who were eager to share their plans and ideas with me of what they had in store for their brothels. It was nice to see that the industry was elevating its status. It was long overdue. Other industries have elevated their status, why not brothels?

Strip clubs used to be thought of as seedy places where no one wanted to be seen entering or leaving. They weren't in the best neighborhoods, often on some dark back street in an industrial zone, with a half-lighted neon sign and a guy standing out front who you just knew was wanted somewhere. Now, many of them are in beautiful buildings with bright lighting. They are quite lavish on the inside, too, with beautifully embellished cigar rooms, bottle service and plush VIP areas. It is quite elite to possess a VIP card to one of these clubs. Now, they are labeled "gentlemen's clubs."

Gaming wasn't always thought of as a "respectable" business, either. Years ago, casinos were smoke-filled gambling dens where the women were loose and liquor flowed freely. They were thought of as a gangster's hangout. Not so today. The casinos being built today are multibillion-dollar resorts. You can see everything on the Las Vegas Strip, from Egyptian pyramids to pirate ships. It is a privilege to be "comped" at these resorts, and people are quick to boast about their comp privileges. Who would have thought those smoke-filled gambling dens would evolve into something that would come with "bragging rights"?

Things in the brothel industry were definitely changing, and it makes me smile to this day to know that I played a part in that change for the better.

A few months passed and the holiday season was right around the corner. It was always sad for me to see the ladies at the brothel during the holidays. The ones who worked during those times didn't seem to mind, though. They really didn't have anywhere else to be, and that was the part that was so sad. They felt they were right where they should be, "home." For some of the ladies, the brothel was the only stability they had ever known. They felt safe and secure there. They knew they would be taken care of should they become ill. Yes, this was home to them, but I couldn't help but feel sad. Naturally, they would never know how I felt, and the house would brim with holiday spirit.

The ladies would decorate the entire brothel. We would put up two huge trees in the parlor for the ladies to decorate. They did a beautiful job. The fireplace in the parlor would be lighted and we would make eggnog. My husband would string lights along the front of the brothel, on the villas, on all the trees, and on the hotel. I would buy gifts for all the ladies, and the kitchen would prepare a special holiday dinner. They were happy; they were home.

One year, one of the ladies came up with a great idea. "Why don't we have a toy drive for the children of Pahrump at our holiday party, Mom?"

"That's a great idea, Cindy!"

From that year on, we had a toy drive at our annual holiday party. Everyone who attended, and we invited everyone, would bring a new, unwrapped gift for a boy or girl. You should have seen all the toys! People would show up with four or five toys. The ladies were very generous as well. They would go shopping on pay days and come back with bags of toys. Each week, when the ladies would get paid, they would have four hours to go into town to do their banking, pay their bills, shop, and take care of whatever they needed. During the holidays, they would buy tons of toys.

The local fire department was kind enough to deliver the toys with the help of the Salvation Army. The first year we had more than three hundred toys. The next year we had more than five hundred. Each year the numbers went up. Firefighters would pull up to the brothel in their fire truck and we would load up the toys. We filled the entire fire truck to where there was absolutely no more room, so they had to bring a trailer to fit all the toys. The Salvation Army would ensure that the children in need would get the toys before the holiday. Not a child in the town of Pahrump would be without a toy.

You know, when people think of brothels, they just don't think of things like this.

Chapter Fourteen

It's Never Enough

There was no doubt about it, things were going well at the brothel. Year after year, the revenues were increasing. Year after year, the quality of the lineups was improving. But the owners in this business were no different from the owners in any other business. They wanted more.

When I began at the brothel, there were twelve employees and it was barely a million-dollar-a-year business. Now there were fifty employees, the brothel had expanded to cover about twenty acres, and had grown into a multimillion-dollar business. Quite an improvement from those three little trailers!

But business is business, and you could never have too much business. The company ventured into other venues that never would have been considered if it weren't for the brothel's success. The corporate offices housed five people when I started. We were like family. Everybody knew one another; I mean really knew one another. We'd have barbecues together, go to concerts and shows. But more importantly, we all got along. There was a genuine concern for one another. There was none of the cutthroat crap that goes on in big companies. No one wanted anyone else's job, no one was jealous of what somewhat else got paid. We were all content with what we had and we were all content with one another. That's the way things should be, but it's like the old saying, "When things seem too good to be true, they probably are."

Things started to change. Believe me, I'm not averse to change. Hell, things had been changing at the brothel ever since I got there. I am all for change, provided the changes are for the better.

The company was growing by leaps and bounds. The corporate offices were bursting at the seams. There were so many people crammed into that office space that it looked more like a warehouse than a corporate office. There were filing cabinets and boxes of records everywhere. You could hardly move. One by one the original five corporate employees dwindled to one. That one was Sam. Sam wasn't his old self anymore, either.

When the first new property was almost completed, I was asked to help. This new property was in the adult industry as well, but it wasn't a brothel. I left the brothel for what I thought was originally going to be a week or two to help get it going. What a mess! There was no way this place would be ready in one or two weeks.

Construction was behind and Shawn was having a fit because for every day this club wasn't open, it was costing him about ten thousand dollars. I met with the construction foreman, who was really a nice guy. It seemed that the reason construction was falling behind was that there was no one on site who could make a decision about anything.

"I'll tell you what, you tell me what you need and I'll make the decision. How does that sound?" I said.

"Sounds like we're finally going to finish this job. Thank God you're here. I've got jobs stacked up behind this one."

So, that is what we did. Item by item, we began knocking things off the list. Now we were getting somewhere!

The place was starting to shape up. Carpet and wall coverings were being installed. The granite was in for the bar. Equipment deliveries were being made daily. Finally, progress. I hoped I could get out of here soon and get back to my brothel. That's when it dawned on me: I really missed that place. What had happened to me? The brothel was like an insane asylum. There wasn't anything "normal" about that job, or most of the people I worked with. I tried to put it into perspective, but that was no use. No matter how many different ways I tried to justify the occurrences that took place at the brothel, there was just no way anyone could possibly miss something like that. Who in their right mind would miss the antics and the drama that occurred there on a daily basis? It was confirmed; I was nuts. Yes, you had to be half-nuts to take that job, and I was overqualified!

Everything was in place at the club and we were scheduled for our inspections. Most went pretty smooth, until we got to the fire inspection. Here we go again. It took five inspections before the fire marshal finally granted us our certificate of occupancy.

I've come to learn that fire marshals take great pleasure in speaking the word "denied." I am certain that this is music to their ears. Now, I don't take what they do lightly. They have a great responsibility. I realize they are solely responsible, once they have given their approval, that the life safety systems they have inspected have met all codes and standards. That is a huge responsibility and I have the utmost respect for that. What I don't understand is why they don't just tell you everything they want on the first inspection. I'm a big girl; give it to me all at once; I can take it. How hard is that?

It took this guy four times to finally spit out everything he wanted. First it was, "You need more emergency lighting in your showroom." We installed it. Then it was, "You need more emergency lighting on your stairway." We installed it. The third time it was, "You need another fire extinguisher." Done. Finally it was, "Your music has to shut down automatically the minute the emergency lighting goes on." Are you kidding me? It took him four days to come up with this? Meanwhile, it was costing Shawn ten thousand dollars a day and I was hearing about it every five minutes.

Okay, easy fixes, right? Oh no, not in my life! The electrical crew was working around the clock. I'm going to have this place open tomorrow, come hell or high water. All the emergency lighting had been installed. It took them all night, but they got it done. The fire extinguisher had been put in place. The contractor told me there was no way he could rewire the sound system in time to comply with the fire marshal's order. "Fine. Then this is what we'll do. We'll hide someone in the sound booth and the minute the emergency lights come on, they will kill the sound."

"Oh, I don't like the sound of that," the contractor said. I could understand his hesitancy; he had his license on the line.

"The sound of what? I didn't say anything."

"Good, because I didn't hear anything."

I was on my own with this covert operation. I got someone who I could trust would keep his mouth shut and hid him in the sound booth. "Remember, as soon as the lights come on, hit the switch and kill the sound."

We got our certificate of occupancy and afterward, the contractor rewired the sound system. He wasn't kidding when he said it couldn't be done by the next day. As I recall, it took them a week to figure out how to get it done, but they got it done. Everybody was happy. The contractor could move on to his next project, Shawn could leave me alone and make new people miserable, and I could go back to my brothel. It was a win for everyone.

Six weeks had elapsed and I was happy to be going back to the brothel. I returned to find that all hell had broken loose. The ladies basically had taken over the brothel. They were calling the shots. The place was out of control.

The brothel was a very vulnerable property. The ladies lived there during their contract period of two or three weeks, so to them, it was home. When people feel comfortable in their environment, they do things they normally wouldn't do. The ladies felt comfortable, and after all, that was our goal. We wanted them to be comfortable in their environment, in their home. But this . . . well, they had become way too comfortable. They were so comfortable that the staff was working for them, following the ladies' directions. Are you kidding me? There were always more ladies on the property than staff members at any given time. It was a property that you could lose control over very quickly. Apparently in six weeks.

I have always had the reputation of saying what I mean and meaning what I say. That was undisputed. The staff, however, did not possess this characteristic. Evidently, in my absence, the ladies intimidated the staff to such a point that the rules and procedures were not being abided by. The ladies were making the rules. Dirty hustling was now allowed; drinking as much as you wanted was now allowed; it was insane!

"Thank God you're here" was the phrase of the day when I walked into the brothel. It came from the staff, not the ladies. It was that whole "When the cat's away, the mice will play" routine. The staff looked terrified; the ladies had that "deer in the headlights" look when I walked in.

"I don't know what happened," the shift manager said. "It was so gradual that no one even noticed it, and then, all of a sudden, we realized the ladies were in control. They were dirty hustling all the time, not signing for their drinks, getting drunk every night in the bar, and making up different names in the lineups. It was crazy. We tried to stop them, but they just wouldn't listen to us. I don't know what happened. Thank God you're back."

I had the shift manager announce over the PA system that all the ladies were to attend a meeting in the dining room with me. Now. As

I watched them on the camera from my office, filing into the dining room, they all had the same posture: head down, shoulders slumped, eyes to the floor.

"What the hell do you think you're doing?"

There was silence. Did I not say that out loud? No one is answering me. I know I said it out loud, because I heard the pictures rattling on the walls. "Somebody better have an answer; don't make me ask you again."

The mom voice is such an awesome tool. It is that special tone that is somehow connected to your eyes. When you use that tone, your eyes automatically get that crazed look in them. It's very powerful.

The ladies' defense was even better. "You know us, Mom. We just had to do something to entertain ourselves while you were gone. We missed you so much. We were so lonely without you. We just had to do something. We didn't mean anything by it."

"Save it," I snapped. A career in the legal field was definitely not in any of their futures. Did they really think that anyone would believe that shit? Did they really think I would believe that shit? And I missed this place? I gotta be nuts. Oh yeah, that was confirmed a few pages back. Right.

It didn't take long before things settled down and were back to "normal," whatever "normal" is at a brothel. For a week or so following my return, the ladies were on their best behavior. There wasn't one argument or incident, nothing. Why couldn't it be like this all the time? Girls; right, got it.

Now that control of the brothel had been retrieved from the ladies, I thought things would run smoothly, at least for a while. I've got to stop thinking! I am just setting myself up for another letdown.

Chapter Fifteen

POLITICS AND COMPETITION

Politics have their role in every industry. Some industries are subjected to internal politics. You know, people jockeying for position; people who would stop at nothing to get his job or her job or your job. Casinos are famous for their internal politics. Changing management regimes in the casino industry are not uncommon. The casino business is all about the numbers, on the casino floor and behind the scenes alike. It is all about winning, for both sides. Gamblers try their luck in hopes of winning. The casino plans its strategy in hopes of winning, too. If the numbers go up year after year, your job is somewhat secure, at least for that coming year. If not, well, then it's time to look for someone who can boost the numbers. Whoever that person may be, you can rest assured he has his own team. So, the higher you are on the food chain, the less job security you have. At the last casino I worked for, I was in a higher management position. I somehow managed to survive four different management regimes before I left the industry. At that time I figured the odds were no longer in my favor. You see, it's all about the numbers.

Then there are industries that are subjected to external politics. These industries are at the mercy of the economy and the current political temperatures; things that are out of their control. The brothels fall into this category.

There was a movement brewing, put into motion by a local politician, to outlaw legal prostitution. A referendum was introduced and found its way onto the ballot. Needless to say, all the brothels in Southern Nevada were concerned. How would you like to have a business whose destiny lies in the hands of the voters, the majority of whom were churchgoing citizens?

The brothel owners were not resting easy, especially ours. They were sitting on a multimillion-dollar investment. That's a lot of money — their money! In a matter of a vote, they could be put out of business, finished.

We had to put together some sort of strategy. The brothels had kept a low profile for years, primarily because of possible political ramifications. Flying under the radar had been the strategy of all the brothels since their inception. Don't make waves; don't call attention to the brothel industry — that was their method of operation and always had been. But we couldn't just do nothing, could we? Nothing doesn't seem to be working for us anymore. There must be something we can do. But what?

We needed a united front. That's it! All the brothel owners would band together. We would pool our resources and together we would stand up and fight. This was war!

The last time there was a brothel vote was in Lincoln County in eastern Nevada. The outcome: Legal prostitution was outlawed. But this was different. In Lincoln County the brothels were fighting among themselves, brothel vs. brothel. The community finally got fed up and voted to outlaw legal prostitution.

Our fight was different. We were not fighting with one another; it wasn't brothel against brothel. The brothels were a united front, a team. But how would we be perceived? Everyone knows that perceptions are people's realities. Would we be perceived as troublemakers or rebels? Would they get fed up as well? Would they vote us out? They could, but would they? Would this be like Custer's last stand? There was one thing everyone agreed on: The risk was huge. What the brothel owners couldn't agree on was whether it was a risk worth taking.

Brothel owners and their representatives sat in meetings for hours on end. People would argue, vehemently, across the table. They were shouting and shaking their fingers. Oh, this wasn't going well at all. As I looked around the room and listened to all that was being said, the thought that kept going through my mind was, Oh shit, it's Lincoln County all over again!

"People, stop. Do you see what is happening here? Our united front is self-destructing!" They all agreed on that, but do you think they could agree on what we should do? You've got to be kidding me!

I have to find a job where there isn't so much chaos. I have to find a job where there isn't so much yelling and screaming and fighting. I have to find a job where people can make a decision. You had one, you idiot! Before you came here, the only problem someone had was deciding what color polish to wear!

Well, while we were busy strategizing and planning and arguing, it became apparent that there were others who were doing the same. Red Hats to the rescue! The Red Hats were irate. They were beside themselves. Shut down the brothels? Over their dead bodies!

While we were fighting and arguing with one another — should we do something, should we do nothing — the Red Hats took action. They wrote letters of protest, they sent e-mails, they attended commission meetings, they even went door to door, dressed up in their purple and red outfits and those marvelous red hats. They were fired up! They were relentless. They were a force to be reckoned with. The last thing you wanted to do was piss off one of those little old Red Hats, and you never wanted to piss them ALL off. Well, it was too late for that. They were ALL pissed off. They weren't going to take this sitting down.

The Red Hats stormed that politician's office and demanded to have a meeting right then and there. "We're not leaving until we have our meeting. We have no place to go. We can wait all day." And wait they did. And they got their meeting. They certainly were women of their word.

The Red Hats created such a stir that the local politician who started this whole mess withdrew his referendum from the ballot. He knew he didn't have what it took to take on all those mad Red Hats. Be afraid; be very afraid.

That local political figure didn't win re-election that year, either. What a shock! That'll teach them. There was no escaping the long arms of the Red Hats.

We all learned something from that experience and that was don't mess with the Red Hats' favorite hangout. "Where the Red Hats meet the Red Lights," remember?

With every election, things got a little more tense at the brothel. With new people running for office, you never knew what their thought processes were regarding brothels. In the legal prostitution field, you are never quite as comfortable as you would like to be. Who could be? Never knowing if your business would be shut down on a whim, your guard had to be constantly up and you always had to be on the top of your game politically. You would rarely find a politician who would publicly support the brothels. Oh, they'll take your money, but public support? Forget about it. I can't recall one political figure who refused a campaign contribution from the brothel. There was no doubt about it, this was one tough business.

During one election year there was a candidate running whose father was a pastor in the community. If he got in, our life would be hell. Well, as luck would have it, the pastor's kid won. Hellooooooo . . . we're talking about my life, remember? Did you think the pastor's kid wouldn't win?

Midnight candlelight vigils were held to try to close down the brothels. You knew that would make the news. Religion and politics, those were two areas I would never approach and now we were right in the thick of both of them. They would pray for our souls. (Well, that might not have been a bad thing.) We were immoral! How could anyone, with a clear conscience, earn a living putting women out as prostitutes?

People, for some reason, think legal prostitution is a form of white slavery. Some illegal prostitution may be, but not legal prostitution. Those ladies work in the industry of their own free will. They aren't forced to work at the brothel. They are independent contractors! They do it for their own reasons, not because we forced them to. Hell, they made as much money as any doctor, except they didn't have an expensive medical education to pay for.

The taxes on brothels were exorbitant. Whether it was property taxes, licensing fees, sheriff's cards or anything associated with the brothels, the taxes seemed to be tripled at least. For example, all independent contractors and employees of the brothel were required to have a sheriff's card, right? All casino employees are required to have sheriff's cards, too. In the casino industry, a sheriff's card is thirty-five dollars for five years. The exact same sheriff's card for a brothel worker is sixty-two dollars and fifty cents per quarter. That's two hundred and fifty dollars for one year. You don't think the brothel's taxes and fees were substantially higher than the rest of America's? That money went into the county's general fund. The brothels didn't get any of it. The taxes from the brothels paid the politicians' salaries! And they took our campaign contributions. Are you nuts? Leave us alone!

Well, the pastor's kid served one term in office and during the latter portion of that term got mixed up in some federal investigation, which preoccupied him with bigger problems and kept him off our backs.

Things had finally settled down in the political arena — for now, anyway — so it was business as usual, right? Yeah, sure.

Meanwhile, prostitution in Las Vegas was running rampant. Many people outside Nevada think prostitution is legal in Las Vegas. It is not. But the image that Las Vegas projects would lead you to believe that it is. Think of "Sin City" and "What Happens in Vegas, Stays in Vegas." The Las Vegas police department doesn't have enough time, resources, or manpower to combat illegal prostitution. They have too many other crimes to deal with. So, prostitution was tolerated there. Don't get me wrong. If a Las Vegas police officer sees a prostitute in action, he will arrest her, but the department rarely sets up any sting operations or takes a proactive approach to busting illegal prostitution.

So, now the brothel had to compete with a rise in illegal prostitution in Las Vegas. The customer base of the brothel was from Las Vegas. Not the Las Vegas residents so much as the tourists who visited. Everybody comes to Vegas. Why not? There's no other place like it in the world. Oh sure, there is gambling most everywhere now, but there is still only one Las Vegas. No other gaming destination can compete.

The brothel was located sixty miles outside of Las Vegas. If someone was looking for companionship and could find it right there in Las Vegas, what would compel him to travel sixty miles for it? Just what I needed, another battle.

I posted a sentence on the home page of our website, "PROSTITUTION IS NOT LEGAL IN LAS VEGAS," in hopes that at least the people visiting the site would be educated. I did some radio interviews, as I had a rapport with the disc jockeys resulting from our annual event, in hopes that I might catch a tourist or two listening while they were sightseeing in their rental car. I knew the casino hosts got girls for their players. Hell, I did it myself when I was in the gaming business. I called the casino hosts at all the hotels (I still kept in touch with my gaming connections) and offered them a percentage of whatever a customer they referred to the brothel spent in an effort to combat my illegal competition. I offered the same to hotel valets, bellhops, you name it. Whatever I could think of, I did.

Word spread quickly among the ladies that prostitution busts weren't a priority in Las Vegas and some of them left to work independently. Most of those who left were ladies who had pimps. Their pimps kept a finger on the pulse of the world of prostitution. The pimps would pull their ladies from the house and put them on the streets in Las Vegas. Now, the pimp would get to keep ALL the money — no more fifty-fifty split with the house. A lot of the ladies did not want to leave the brothel. Unfortunately, their opinions and desires didn't count, not where a pimp was concerned. They either followed orders or they would suffer severe consequences. I felt bad for them. If they didn't leave, they would be beaten. If they did leave and got busted for illegal prostitution, they would be beaten. They were in a no-win situation and were too scared to even think about getting out of it.

The number of cabs and limos bringing customers to the brothel was declining. They, too, knew they didn't have to leave Las Vegas to accommodate their customers.

In an effort to sway drivers to bring customers to the brothel, we started hosting "Drivers' Parties" in Las Vegas for the cab and limo drivers. We would have free food and drawings for prizes. We gave away thousands of dollars in prizes, including vacations, televisions, all sorts of electronics, brothel parties, anything we could think of to buy their loyalty. Just like anything else, with some drivers it worked, with others it didn't. But we knew we had to keep trying. We put gift bags together and each time a driver would bring a customer to the brothel, he would receive a gift bag, in addition to the commission that the brothel paid.

I had a calendar made featuring the ladies of the brothel. Twelve ladies, one for each month, were picked to be featured in the calendar. Other ladies were on the front cover and back cover. Each year different ladies would be portrayed in the calendar. We put the calendars in the drivers' gift bags and sold them in the gift shop. When people would buy a calendar and see a lady from the calendar sitting in the bar, they would ask for an autograph. The ladies would gladly sign the calendars; they felt like celebrities. They would get very creative with their signatures. "Cum see me." "Thanks for cumming." "Ya'll cum back now, ya hear." The customers loved it. We had customers bring their calendars with them whenever they came to the brothel in hopes of gaining another autograph. The calendars became prized possessions.

All cab drivers and limousine drivers were paid a commission, based on a percentage of what the customer spent at the brothel. The more the customer spent, the more the driver was paid. All the brothels did that to entice drivers to bring customers to their brothel. It was a struggle. Our brothel did have an advantage that none of the others had: We served food. The other brothels just served food to their ladies, but we had a restaurant. We fed all the drivers for free. They loved it. While their customer was partying, they could relax, have a nice meal, and drool over the beautiful scenery.

Some customers paid for their driver to party as well. That was not uncommon. I remember, from time to time, a driver would insist that he be paid a commission on his party, in addition to his customer's party. I would try to explain to the driver that we do not pay a commission on the driver's party. They couldn't grasp that idea. So, I would just break it down in terms that they could grasp. "Why would I pay you to party with one of my ladies?"

"Oh, I see what you mean."

No matter what the obstacle, politics, illegal prostitution, or pimps pulling ladies out of the house, we seemed to overcome it. I just kept coming up with new ideas and new tactics.

One Saturday, James and my husband were installing new cameras for me. After they had finished, I bought them a beer and we sat in the bar. While the three of us were sitting there, James had an eight-foot piece of conduit leaning on the table next to him. One of the ladies, Dixon, came over to our table and asked James if he could stand up that piece of conduit. He did, and Dixon used it as a pole and started pole dancing. She captured the attention of everyone in the bar. Thoughts began rushing through my mind. Why don't we get rid of that stupid golf game that no one plays, clear out that corner, and put in a stage with a pole?

How often does a guy go into a strip club, watch the girls dance, and wish they could do more? Here, they could! It was genius. My husband and James must have been having the same thought I was, because we all just looked at one another, smiled, and nodded.

The next Saturday, James and my husband built the stage, mirrored the two walls by the stage, and installed lighting. I ordered the pole and before you knew it, it was done.

The ladies danced, the guys drooled, and before too long they were being escorted back to the ladies' rooms. We didn't have any laws, as the strip clubs in Las Vegas do, regulating how far a dancer had to be from a customer, or not allowing a dancer to grind on a customer or put her boobs in his face. We had free rein. Now, when guys got the urge to take it to the next level, well, we were there to accommodate them. How great was that?

There was always something that would occur to swing the pendulum back in our favor. A prostitute in Las Vegas was found strangled in one of the hotels, a story that headlined the nightly news and newspapers. That scared the other illegal prostitutes and they would then look to work in a legal house as a safe haven. Anyone looking for work in a house tended to call our brothel first. We were the best, by far, and had an unsurpassed reputation. We not only had the nicest facility, but the best reputation in the treatment of the ladies, the best reputation of the clientele, and most important, the best reputation for making money . . . big money. Being the best allowed me to be very selective in the ladies I would hire at the brothel.

I turned down some drop-dead-gorgeous women. Looks alone wouldn't land you the job. You had to possess what I called "the package." The package was: looks, personality, attitude, nice smile, friendliness, approachable, and commitment to offer customer service at the excellence level. With so many ladies coming from all over the world, I couldn't interview everyone personally. The ladies who came from the Las Vegas area, I would meet in my office. With the others, I would conduct interviews with them over the phone. Call me crazy, but it is true: You can hear a smile over the phone. Really, I kid you not. My phone interviews were relatively simple, and once I determined that the lady was at least twenty-one years old and had no outstanding warrants, the interview went something like this: "So, sweetheart, tell me about yourself." Based on what she had to say, and how she said it, I could pretty much determine if she possessed "the package."

I didn't want all the ladies to look like Barbie dolls. Oh, they were all pretty, but some weren't as pretty as others. A lot of men are intimidated by really beautiful women. You had to have some ladies who looked like "the girl next door," too.

I held a meeting with the ladies each week. In those meetings we went over any issues they had, any issues I or the staff had, marketing, and customer service training. The meetings were a forum for the ladies. If the food wasn't up to standard, I wanted to know and I would correct it. If the tanning bed, their computers, or anything wasn't working properly, I wanted to know and I would correct it. If they had any complaints about how they were being treated, I wanted to know and I would correct it. Of course, it was my forum as well. Should they be doing something that wasn't up to our standards, I wanted them to know so they could correct it.

We would discuss marketing. Now, you might be thinking, what could the ladies possibly do from a marketing standpoint? Well, there was plenty. When a lady booked in to the brothel, we would set up an e-mail account for her and customers could contact her directly through our website. We would discuss how to properly answer those e-mails. When they answered e-mails, they were marketing themselves to the customer. By law, prices could not be quoted over the Internet; that was considered soliciting. They could give a price range, but could not quote specific numbers. They could write "high four digits" or "low five digits," but they could never quote a price. The terminology they used was an important marketing factor. Which one do you think someone would pay more for: "I'll fuck you until you come" or "I will satisfy your every desire until you are groaning with delight"? Marketing was a topic at every meeting.

Customer service is an area where no one can top out. There is always room to improve customer service, regardless of how good you might be. The best in the business will tell you that. Customer service was the most important aspect of the ladies' jobs. I'm not talking about customer satisfaction; they always satisfied the customer. Customer service, however, at times had to be delicate, particularly if the lady and her customer couldn't reach an agreement during the negotiation. You have to remember, the customer had come to a brothel. If you went to a brothel and couldn't reach an agreement with a lady on the price, how would you feel? Nothing says rejection more than going to a brothel and not being able to get laid! It was a very difficult situation for the customer. His ego had been bruised, not to mention his self-esteem being shot to shit. Those situations must be handled very delicately. He needed to be built up, reassured, his self-esteem had to be elevated. That was the job of the lady who picked up the "walk." She had to do damage control, in addition to the negotiation. I must say, the ladies were very good at restoring a guy's self-esteem. They always knew the right things to say and the right way to say them.

Every week the meetings were a little different. You had different ladies in the house, different situations that took place, etc. But one thing would remain constant. I would end each meeting the same way: "You are all, indeed, very beautiful, but the bottom line, ladies, is no one wants to spend time with a beautiful bitch." And that was the reality of it.

Who would ever think that so much strategy and planning would go on just to run a brothel? The whole industry was more or less like an endless game of chess. Consider: the ladies and their drama; politics and the drama that brought; strategizing to have just the right mix of ladies in the lineup week after week; the everyday crap that you had to do to run the business. The job could be quite a handful at times.

When people think of brothels, the first thought they have is "sex for money." That may be true with illegal prostitution, but legal prostitution is a business just like any other. It's really no different than working for a hotel, casino, or restaurant, from a business point of view. The brothel business, just like other businesses, has to comply with labor laws, health department rules and regulations (probably more so in the brothel business), the Internal Revenue Service, and many other regulatory agencies. Payroll has to be done, administrative duties, accounting . . . it's a business, a real, legitimate business.

Chapter Sixteen

STAFF TROUBLES

When people think of brothels, they think of the working girls. But there are many people behind the scenes responsible for making the operation a success. Those people are no different from you or me. (Okay, well, maybe just you. I'll admit I am a little different than most.) They have spouses, children, mortgages, and a job. Their job just happens to be at a brothel.

Staffing at the brothel, just like at any other business, is an ongoing problem. Keep in mind that there are factors the brothel must deal with that most other industries don't. One factor was that we were geographically challenged. We were on the outskirts of a rural town. The brothels were not permitted to be in the center of town; they had to outside of town; you know, in the middle of nowhere. The labor force wasn't as strong in Pahrump as it was in other places, such as Las Vegas.

Another factor was that we were a brothel. Not everyone would consider even stepping into a brothel, much less working in one. There always will be that segment of society that would not be caught dead in such a place. So, with a weak labor force coupled with the fact that we were a brothel, we often felt we were scraping the bottom of the labor pool.

Now, we all know that people put their best foot forward when job hunting, right? They dress the right way, they say the right things, and they appear to be genuinely interested in working. So you hire them.

They learn their new job in a fairly reasonable amount of time and seem to fit in. Then they get comfortable and the problems start.

They start to take notice of how much the ladies earn. After all, the shift managers handled the monetary transactions. Over the years we had some shift managers with some very big mouths. They, for some reason, felt they needed to share that information with everyone they worked with. It didn't matter what department they worked in, housekeeping, security, bartenders, whoever would listen; and you know that if somebody is talking about somebody else, you don't have a problem finding an audience.

There were those employees who wanted some of the ladies' money, too. Why should the ladies have so much money and I have so little? That was the way some staff members saw things. They wanted their share. We cater to those ladies; we are entitled to some of their money was the staff's reasoning. They couldn't steal it anymore. No, there were too many checks and balances in place now. They had to find another way to finagle money out of the ladies.

The ladies were not allowed to tip any of the staff, so that was out. I had put a policy of "no tipping the staff" in place in an effort to keep an even playing field among the ladies. Tipping the staff would only create favoritism toward particular ladies. The lady who tipped more would be treated better. We couldn't have that. Also, knowing how the ladies operated as well as I did, they could start tipping security so they could smuggle in drugs; tipping housekeeping so that if they found drugs or money in their rooms, they wouldn't say anything; tipping the bartenders for extra drinks. The possibilities were endless.

I learned over the years that the staff, at times, could be as creative as the ladies. Some staff members would offer to pick up items that the ladies needed from the store on their way to work. The ladies were so grateful. They would take money out of their petty cash and give it to the employee to pay for the purchase. Since the ladies were not permitted to have any money in their rooms, we set up a petty cash account for each lady and put any money they brought to the brothel in their petty cash account. If any money was found in any lady's room, it was assumed she was stealing and she would be thrown out of the brothel, never to return.

The ladies used their petty cash to buy drinks, if a customer didn't buy them for them, to buy cigarettes, and to buy clothes. Since the ladies had only four hours out of the brothel once a week, I would have clothing vendors come in and the ladies could shop while at the brothel. That's what they would use their petty cash for.

Now, some staff members were offering to pick things up for them, which would give the ladies more time on their day out to take care of other things they needed to get done. How nice. Yeah, right.

I just happened to be at the shift manager's desk one day when the oncoming shift manager came in with a bag from one of the department stores. She picked up the phone and paged Jasmine to come to the office. "Here you go, sweetie. I picked up what you needed from the store."

"Oh, thank you so much." Jasmine took the bag and went to her room.

I asked the shift manager what Jasmine needed. "Oh, she needed tampons, so I told her I would pick them up for her."

"She just came up to you and told you she needed tampons?"

"Yes."

Later on, in casual conversation, I asked Jasmine how the shift manager knew she needed tampons. "Oh, she asks me every day if I need her to pick up anything from the store, and yesterday I told her I needed tampons.

"Did you take money out of your petty cash?"

"Yes."

I checked the log sheet on Jasmine's petty cash. The ladies were required to sign the sheet, attached to their petty cash envelope, for each deposit and withdrawal. Jasmine had withdrawn forty dollars yesterday.

While Jasmine was having her dinner, I stopped to chat with her. "Sweetheart, did you take forty dollars out of your petty cash for the tampons?"

"Yes."

"Did you get any change?"

"No."

No, are you kidding me? What, are those tampons made of gold?

"We never get any change."

"What do you mean, never? Has anyone ever gone to the store for you before?"

"Oh yes, a lot of the shift managers go to the store for a lot of the ladies, but no one ever gets any change."

"How do you know how much money to give to the shift manager?"

"They tell us."

"Sweetheart, do you think tampons cost forty dollars?"

"No, but they tell us we have to give them money for gas and for their time. You know, gas is expensive."

Okay, the ladies aren't working at the brothel because they just missed out at a job at NASA, but they were smarter than that. Why would they give them so much money?

That's how I learned that some staff members were essentially running their own business inside the brothel. It wasn't just the shift managers, it was the hostesses, bartenders, kitchen workers, housekeepers. They were all in on the action. So, I instituted yet another policy. As if the crap that went on with the ladies and the politics wasn't enough, now the staff, too? I don't have enough aggravation in my life? Are you kidding me?

Chapter Seventeen

ANOTHER NEW PROJECT

It was about a year after I helped open the new business in Las Vegas when the company's second endeavor was approaching completion. "Can you come to Vegas and help me get this property up and running?" Shawn asked.

I knew I shouldn't have answered the phone. Too bad we couldn't get caller ID on a multi-line phone system! "Sure, why not." I had a year to recover from the last one; I figured I should be good to go.

So once again, I was commuting to Las Vegas every day from Pahrump. Didn't I move to Pahrump to avoid commuting? Yeah, how is that working for you? I've always had a knack for being at the wrong place at the wrong time. With my luck, when my ship finally comes in, I'll be at the airport.

The new business was a totally new concept in adult entertainment. It was a strip club, nightclub and after-hours club all housed under one roof. There would be something to appeal to everyone. I was not too familiar with the "after hours" portion of the business. Those clubs didn't get started until four o'clock in the morning — way past my bedtime. At my age, I had forgotten that four o'clock came around twice a day.

The same construction foreman who built the other business was building this one. I walked on to the site and he yelled from the other side of the building, "Is that my favorite madam I see?" I walked over and we hugged. It was nice to see him again. "I can't tell you how glad I am to see you," he said.

"Did you miss me that much?" I asked.

"Hell yeah. You thought that last one was bad; wait until you sink your teeth into this one."

"What's going on?"

"The last time we worked together, I couldn't find anyone to make a decision, not until you got there. Remember? Well, this time there's three of them who think they're the boss and they can't agree on anything, so I still can't get a decision. And wait 'til you meet these three. Oh, you're gonna have fun with this group."

Great.

I walked over to the trailer that served as the temporary office space. There was a meeting going on. Do you remember when you were in school and walked into your classroom late, how everybody stopped what they were doing and looked at you? That's what they did.

There were three guys, all dressed in three-piece suits, and four other guys.

"Can I help you?" one of the suits asked with a smug tone.

"I'm from the brothel and I'm actually here to help *you*, but thanks for asking."

Three-piece suits . . . are you kidding me? This place was under construction! Who the hell were they trying to impress, the electricians? The foreman was right; I was going to have fun with this group.

The meeting wrapped up and I introduced myself to the three suits. They were all bosses. One was the boss of the nightclub, one was the boss of the strip club, and one was the boss of the after-hours club. Naturally, they were fighting over which segment of the business was more important, which would make their job more important as well.

"I'll tell you what, while you three figure out who is the top dog, I will work with the foreman and get your club built. How does that sound?"

"That sounds like a plan to me," they agreed. Who hired these kids? And believe me, they were kids. I had outfits older than they were.

I found my favorite foreman. "Good news. You are I are working together again. The three stooges have more important issues to resolve, so it's just you and me."

"That is good news. Where did these guys come from anyway?"

"I have no idea. Don't know, don't want to know," I said, and I meant it.

So again, we got busy checking off items on the punch list. It was a pretty good-sized club, but nowhere near big enough to house all those egos. I'm not sure Las Vegas was big enough to house all those egos. Oh well, not my problem. I just wanted to get this thing built and opened and go back to my brothel. There were the usual routine hold-ups: late deliveries, things on back order, wrong items sent. Construction was moving along, so I decided to check on the three stooges to see if they had made any progress.

They were sitting around in the trailer. One was kicked back in his chair with his feet up on the desk. One was talking on his BlackBerry and the other was flirting with the secretary. I walked into the trailer and the one suit almost fell backwards out of his chair. "We've heard a lot about you," the suit in the chair said.

Well, that could go either way. "Really. Anything good?" I asked.

"Oh, it was all good." A suck-up in a suit . . . perfect.

"Your club is scheduled to open in approximately two weeks. Have any of you trained your staff on the accounting system, point-of-sale procedures, anything like that?

"No" was the response from all three of them.

"Are you planning to train your staff sometime before you actually open?"

They looked at one another with that look that I just love: deer in the headlights. "Let me ask you something. Do any of you know the accounting system, point-of-sale procedures, anything?"

"No" again from all three. You've got to be kidding!

I trained the three stooges and I trained their staffs. They didn't have one written procedure, so I did that as well. By the time I would have gotten through explaining everything to them, it was quicker and easier just to do it myself.

I had been there about a week when Shawn called to see how everything was going. "You have Manny, Moe, and Jack-Off here and you want to know how it's going?" I asked. I told him my thoughts about the three suits and he laughed. Sure, he could laugh, he wasn't spending every day with them. I, however, wanted to strangle them. How did I get mixed up in all this crap? Shawn: It was all his fault. Damn, he was so hard to say no to.

In the lobby of the club was a gigantic martini glass where there would be a girl lounging in the water, welcoming the guests. The concept was great, but no one thought of feeding water to the glass. "How do they propose to get water in that thing?" I asked the foreman.

"I have no idea," he said, "I gave them a bid on a water supply system but Shawn said it was too expensive."

"So now what?" I asked.

"Your guess is as good as mine."

I asked Shawn about getting water to the martini glass. "Just dump buckets of water in it," he suggested.

Are you kidding me? That thing was huge. "You're telling me you're going to have people dumping buckets of water in it, right in the middle of the lobby, where all the guests will be coming through?"

"Yeah, don't worry, it will be fine."

The club opened one week later. Shawn and I ran around the place like lunatics. I was helping the staff with the point of sale and credit cards, running from the front desk to the bar to the VIP lounge and back again. Shawn had a radio and was assisting security. Two of the three suits were actually hosting the customers and the third one, well, he was flirting with the cocktail waitresses and dancers. Shawn was fit to be tied.

"Can you believe this shit?" Shawn asked me.

"I tried to tell you but you thought it was funny, remember?"

About two hours into the night, Shawn had had enough and fired suit number three right then and there. The other two suits didn't make it through the first year.

Meanwhile, Shawn's idea of dumping buckets of water in the martini glass was a disaster. The place was crowded; there was water all over the marble floor; the girl looked like a drowned rat; and on top of it all, she was freezing! It was cold water and it was December!

Shawn came to me and said, "This isn't working. You have to find a better system. The buckets of water aren't working."

I have to find a better system? This wasn't my club, but apparently it was my problem.

"Well, there's nothing I can do tonight, but I'll get on it first thing in the morning. In the meantime, we have to get that girl out of the glass. She's turning blue!"

The opening of the club was a success. The place was packed, the opening staff did a good job considering they had only one week of training, and the guests all seemed to enjoy themselves.

The next day I addressed the martini glass. Not only did they not give any thought to how to get the water in, they didn't give any thought to how to get the water out. The foreman went to the hardware store and bought a pump and two hundred feet of hose. I went to the fabric store and bought yards of black velvet and foam.

I lined the bottom of the glass with foam, draped the black velvet, and placed black velvet pillows on top of that. I sprinkled red rose pedals, silk ones, all around the pillows and fabrics. Perfect! Another problem solved.

My work there was done and it was time for me to head back to the brothel. I couldn't wait to get back. I had had my fill of egos, enough to last me a lifetime! I needed to get back to the simple life; back to the life of prostitutes and pimps.

Chapter Eighteen

TEAM BUILDING, DREAM BUILDING

It took quite a while to work through all the staffing problems, but finally I put together a really good team. They were a true team, working together to achieve a common goal. This team knew how important it was to treat the ladies fairly and with respect. This team knew how important it was to make the customer's dreams come true. This team grasped what customer service was all about. I couldn't believe it: Finally, I found people who shared the same philosophy that I did.

And the ladies, well, they couldn't have been happier. For one thing, they were no longer being nickel-and-dimed to death by scheming staff members.

Customers would call just to talk to the shift managers because the service they received when they visited the brothel was beyond their expectations. They felt a connection with the shift managers who had taken care of them so well during their stay. People couldn't believe how well they were treated, especially at a brothel.

Our regular clientele was growing. The hotel had a regular clientele of its own. Sure, the majority of the hotel guests partied in the brothel, but there also was that segment of guests who stayed at the hotel and never partook of the brothel services. To them it was just a resort with beautiful rooms, spa, pool, and a staff that treated them like royalty. It was hard to believe that people would rather drive an hour out of Las Vegas just to stay there. We didn't have a casino, why on Earth would they do that?

I came to learn that staying at the brothel was a novelty to them. Although they may not have used the services, they would go home and boast to their friends about how they spent the night at a brothel. "Let them figure out what I did all night," was their devilish comment, over and over again.

There was no other brothel in the world where you could spend the night, at least without one of the ladies. Not only could you be anyone you wanted to be while you were at the brothel, but you could be anyone you wanted to be once you got home. Customers would flaunt their receipts from their hotel stay as "proof" that they spent the night at a brothel. Yet another parallel to the casino industry: We had bragging rights, too!

Those who stayed at the hotel and didn't use the brothel services were a little different from your average Joe. They seemed to be extremely introverted. You know the type: They never made eye contact and always walked hunched over, looking at the floor, exhibiting no self confidence whatsoever. They would walk through the property hoping not to be noticed. But our customer service was at the excellence level, so we noticed them, we smiled at them, we spoke to them, and we let them know how glad we were that they were here. And they would book back in, again and again.

As time passed, I would notice them walking a little taller, smiling as they passed by, and speaking. What was this? I would chat with them and get to know them a bit. Before long, they would share parts of their lives with me.

That's how I learned about the bragging rights. I remember one guy in particular. His name was Dewey. That doesn't surprise you, does it? He looked like a Dewey. Dewey came to my office one day and asked to speak with me.

"Can I close the door, madam?"

"Of course, Dewey, how can I help you?"

"You know, this is my third visit here and I've got to tell you something."

"Is everything all right?"

"Oh, yes, it couldn't be better. You know, I'm not what one would consider a ladies' man."

I never would have guessed! His name was Dewey, for heaven's sake!

"Well, every time I leave here and go home, I tell all my friends that I've spent the night at a brothel. Of course, they don't believe me, so I show them my receipt. I've got to tell you, I've more or less become a hero to all my friends."

As he was speaking, I was imagining a whole pack of Deweys drooling over his receipt, giggling, laughing, and snorting. Trying to maintain composure and professionalism, I found myself chewing a hole through the side of my mouth.

Dewey was a small-framed, skinny guy with short, mousy brown hair, and brown eyes. He wore glasses, really thick ones. His posture wasn't the best and his choice of clothing was even worse. Dewey wore corduroy pants (didn't they go out of style in the '70s?), a short-sleeved collared shirt with a pocket, complete with a pocket protector, and dirty sneakers. You weren't going to see any photos of Dewey in *GQ* anytime soon!

"Well, that's wonderful, Dewey. Everyone needs a hero," I said.

"Well, I am feeling bad because I am lying to my friends. You know, lying is bad and I hate lying to anyone. So, I've made a decision. I'm going to do it."

"Do what?"

"You know, it!"

"Oh, well, that's quite a big decision, Dewey."

"I have a problem, though, and I thought maybe you could help me."

"What's the problem?"

"I've never done it before, at least not with a woman. I normally do it by myself."

What a shock! "Oh, I see." (I mean I really see; I was picturing all of this in my mind and I couldn't stop! I really don't want to know Dewey that well, or anyone, for that matter.)

"I feel so close to you, madam. You were the first person ever who really seemed to care about me."

"Well, I do care, Dewey, so tell me, what can I do to help?" (I am really curious now, because if he says what I think he's going to say, I'm going to knock him right off of the chair.)

"Maybe you could give me some advice." He's lucky — he can remain in the chair. "I mean, I don't know what to do. I'm thirty-seven years old and I've never even kissed a woman, except for my mom. Can you help me?"

My mind was racing. I had a million thoughts running through my head. I'm sure Dewey was not the only guy like this. How many others were there? Well, there were Dewey's friends, although I don't know how many friends he had. But the point was, Dewey was not alone. I'm sure there were a lot of guys out there just like him. Can you imagine? Thirty-seven years old and not possessing the confidence or self-esteem to even approach a woman? How lonely an existence was that?

"Okay, Dewey. Here's what we'll do. Do you have a particular type of girl that you like better than others? You know, blondes over brunettes, short over tall. What is your preference, Dewey?"

"It doesn't matter. Anyone who would, maybe, just wouldn't mind a guy like me too much."

Okay, now he was breaking my heart. Dewey was a bit of a dork; all right, quite a bit, but he wasn't a monster. He was a person, for cryin' out loud. Flesh and blood, just like you and me, with feelings and needs, just the same as you and me. Oh, the poor guy!

"Dewey, any of the ladies here would love to spend some time with you. You're a nice guy."

Just then I caught myself . . . "nice" was the word you used when you couldn't think of anything else to say about someone. Think about it. How many times have you said, "Oh, but she's really nice" or, "Yeah, but he's so nice." Nice, it was a safe word; a safety net.

"How about having a lineup and picking out the lady that you like best?"

"Oh, no, I couldn't do that, I couldn't pick a lady. I don't want to hurt anyone else's feelings."

Of course not. What was I thinking?

Actually, many customers felt they would hurt the other ladies' feelings by not picking them out of a lineup. A lot of customers did not realize that this was a business for the ladies, that their personal feelings had nothing to do with anything. The ladies were professionals. It wasn't any different than buying a Dodge over a Ford. Nobody's feelings got hurt, it was just about preferences; it was just business.

"How about this, Dewey. In the bar there is a television with photos of the ladies who are in the current lineup. Why don't you take a look at that and let me know which lady you like the best? I'll buy you an O'Douls and you let me know when you have found someone. Okay?"

Dewey didn't drink . . . hell, Dewey didn't do anything.

"Do you think I could have a beer? I really think I'm going to need one."

Dewey went to the bar and I bought him a beer. Thirty minutes later, Dewey came back to my office.

"Madam, I think I found someone."

"Great. Who is it?"

"Shayla."

Shayla was a tall, striking brunette with a short bobbed haircut and bangs. Her dark hair framed her face and she had beautiful green eyes. Shayla was very slim and had huge boobs. Dewey, you devil!

"Okay, Dewey, have a seat on the couch, make yourself comfortable, and I'll get Shayla for you."

I went to Shayla's room, knocked on the door, and walked in. Shayla was lying on her bed, listening to her iPod, and entertaining herself with her vibrator.

"Hi, Mom! I was just spending some time with my little friend."

"Sweetheart, you can put your little friend away. I have the real thing for you." I told Shayla all about Dewey.

"You mean that nerdy little guy who stays in the hotel?"

"Yes, that's him."

"Oh, I can give him something he'll never forget!"

"I'm sure you can, but go easy on him. He's never done it before, so be gentle. Don't scare him and don't use your little friend. He hardly has any self-esteem now. I would hate for him to think he wasn't as good as your little friend!"

Shayla went to the parlor and whisked Dewey back to her room. About an hour later the party ended. When Dewey came out he was grinning like the Cheshire cat. Shayla was grinning, too! Shayla came to my office all excited. "Mom! Dewey was incredible!"

Incredible? I thought he's never done it before. "I thought he was a virgin."

"He was. But you know how those computer nerds are; they're smart. I would show him how to do something, where to put his hands and where to put his fingers, and he would listen and learn. He's really a quick learner, Mom. He was even better than my little friend!"

When Dewey checked out of the hotel to go home, he stopped by my office. "Madam, I can't thank you enough for all your help. I feel like a new man." I'm sure he did.

"I look forward to seeing you again soon, Dewey."

"Oh, you will. I can't wait to get home and tell all my friends." Okay, so he was not that new of a man, at least not yet.

About a month later, Dewey checked back in to the hotel.

"Dewey, is that you?" I asked.

"Hello, madam. I'm so glad to be back."

Dewey had undergone some sort of an extreme makeover. He wore jeans that fit him well, a sporty golf shirt, and nice, clean shoes. No pocket and no pocket protector. He wasn't wearing his glasses either.

"Dewey, where are your glasses?"

"I had laser surgery done and I don't wear them anymore," he said. His hair was longer and combed straight back. I even noticed a hint of styling gel. Dewey was looking pretty sharp!

Dewey partied with two ladies on that trip, one of them being Shayla again. He and Shayla even partied in a villa!

As Dewey was leaving, he caught me walking through the bar. "Madam, I just wanted to thank you again, for everything. You changed my life. People notice me now and pay attention to me. I got a promotion at work, I moved out of my mom's house, and I feel like I'm living for the first time in my life. You've made my dreams come true. I'll never forget you."

I gave Dewey a hug and kissed him on his cheek. "Take care, Dewey, I hope to see you soon."

As Dewey left I couldn't help but smile. What a great feeling, giving someone a new lease on life, so to speak. I hope the other Deweys out there find their way to the brothel. How many other dreamers were out there just like Dewey? There's no telling what we could do!

The ladies of the brothel did not judge a person based on their looks, as we, as a society, tend to do. It was a business and everyone was a potential customer. Therefore, they were all treated the same . . . well. The magic of walking into a brothel is that it doesn't matter what you look like, what kind of car you drive, what type of job you have. The only thing that matters is that you are there, and our job is to show you just how happy we are that you are here. We were dream makers. We would capture your fantasies and deliver them with seduction. That's what it's all about.

As I walked into my office, my phone was ringing. "Yes, this is the madam."

"I am an author, and I am writing a book of diaries of women across America, and I would like to know if you would be interested in submitting something for my book?"

Why not?

"Just keep a diary of one day, any day. The subject matter is twenty-four hours of true-life stories."

She gave me her e-mail address and told me to e-mail my diary to her. True-life stories? Who would believe any of the shit that goes on in twenty-four hours of my life?

So, I kept a diary for the next twenty-four hours. I signed and faxed all the releases and e-mailed off my diary. After that, I didn't give it a second thought.

A year later a package arrived for me at the brothel. I opened it and there it was: her book. And there I was, on page seventy-one! I was in print, in a book! I couldn't wait to tell all my friends. At that moment, thoughts of Dewey flooded my brain. Okay, I'm not going to tell all my friends. I'll just take it home and strategically place it on my coffee table. When friends see it and ask, I'll simply say, "Oh, that's just a book I'm in," very nonchalantly. A much better approach.

Despite the daily drama, the brothel was a fun place to work. All the staff members enjoyed their jobs. It was a relaxed, comfortable, family type of atmosphere. Everyone got along and a lot of friendships were made outside the workplace. There was never a problem getting another employee to cover a shift when someone went on vacation. They would watch one another's animals or kids or both when someone went out of town. The turnover of employees had slowed to a snail's pace.

I hired this one shift manager who was probably in her late twenties, maybe early thirties. She learned the job fast and the ladies really liked her. She was working out great as our graveyard shift manager. Then she called me one night, at the beginning of her shift, in tears. She was sobbing so hard I couldn't understand a word she was saying. Finally, she calmed down enough that I could understand her.

"I have to quit. I don't want to quit, I really love this job, but I have to quit."

"Why do you have to quit?"

"My parents found out I was working here and they said they would disown me if I didn't quit."

Can you imagine that? Disowning your daughter because she works in the office at a brothel? I could have better understood it if they discovered their daughter was a working girl, but she worked in the office. You can't become a prostitute by osmosis!

I remember when one shift manager's husband was offered a job out of state and they had to move. She was crying when she gave her notice to me. Crying, can you believe it? She really loved her job, but mostly taking care of the ladies. That was the hardest part of the job to walk away from. Those ladies, despite all their antics, tantrums, drama, and chaos, had a way of worming their way into your heart.

When people think of prostitutes, they think "hookers" or "whores." I really hate the "w" word. Those who use that word don't stop to think that the ladies are people, too. Those ladies are someone's daughter, granddaughter, aunt, niece, sister . . . even someone's mom. They are someone to somebody. They are no different than any one of us. They have chosen a line of work that many people do not approve of. But what they are not given credit for is that they chose to do this line of work legally. They went through the time and expense of licensing and medical tests for their safety as well as the safety of their customers. They forfeited fifty percent of their earnings for the overhead of a clean and safe facility to work in. These were all conscious decisions made by prostitutes who chose to work in legal houses. They were law-abiding citizens who paid taxes on their earnings. They contributed to the economy. I don't know of any "hooker" or "whore" who does any of that.

I have never been a fan of illegal prostitution. Hell, I didn't know I was a fan of legal prostitution until I was introduced to it. Always being open-minded and nonjudgmental has given me the ability to look at things a little differently, a little more realistically, I suppose.

The ladies who worked in the brothel were indeed dream makers. They weren't giving fifty-dollar blow jobs in someone's back seat or giving twenty-dollar hand jobs in an alley. They fulfilled fantasies. They took you to heights you've always dreamed about experiencing. They role-played and pampered and catered.

And the customers who came to the brothel were, for the most part, successful members of society. They weren't derelicts who couldn't get laid anywhere else. They were people who were looking for something a bit more: more exciting, more daring, more intriguing, more thrilling.

That was particularly true with the couples who visited the brothel. Many couples were interested in exploring sexual fantasies. What would our society think, hell, what would you think if friends approached you and your husband about the possibility of exploring a new sexual experience? I think most would look for new friends. But there is a segment of society that possesses a freethinking spirit, an openness, a sexual freedom, and the brothel offered a venue for that segment.

When people think of brothels, they think of sex everywhere, orgies, sex wherever you turn. But you'll see more action in a strip club than you would ever see at a brothel. Don't forget, we used to do tours, tours that were mostly made up of senior citizens. Do you think senior citizens would walk into a place where, the minute you walked in, there was nothing but sexual activity everywhere? Of course not!

During the tours I would have to remind everyone to please remain quiet while walking through the hallway because we had parties taking place at the time.

"You have parties going on right now?" I would be asked.

"Yes."

The common response was, "I don't hear a thing. I would never have guessed that anything was going on."

I suppose people thought they would hear nonstop moaning and groaning once they entered the brothel. All the rooms were sound-proofed, which was another way we protected the privacy of the customers. Everything at the brothel took place behind closed doors.

Summer was a tough time for the brothel. The desert temperatures would be so extreme that travel slowed down dramatically. There were very few conventions in Las Vegas during the summer months and that took its toll on the brothel business as well. I felt I had to do something to overcome the adverse conditions, but who was I to take on Mother Nature? I was the madam, that's who! I decided, so what if the temperatures outside are well over a hundred degrees, let's have snow parties!

I ordered a snow machine and a foam machine. I had Fernando install them in the Dungeon. I turned them on and shut the door. I gathered up all the ladies. "I'm going to show you something and then I want you to get on the Internet, on all the boards, and invite everyone to party with you . . . in the snow."

I opened the door and the ladies started squealing like children on Christmas morning. The foam machine had spilled a blanket of foam all over the dungeon floor. It was about four inches thick and looked just like snow. The snow machine was blowing snowflakes and it looked like a blizzard in there.

"Mom, how did you do that? That's amazing."

The ladies ran through the room, throwing foam on one another, while the flakes from the snow machine clung to their hair. It was winter in July!

"Okay, ladies, play time is over. We have work to do. Let's tell everyone about the winter wonderland party you have in store for them."

I posted photos on our website and the ladies got busy posting on the Internet. No more dreaming about cooler months in the middle of the summer, in the middle of the desert, anymore. With air conditioning, foam, and snow, we could make that dream come true!

One day I received a call from a sky-diving team from Arizona. "Madam, I have kind of a peculiar question for you."

Peculiar. If he only knew what some of my phone conversations consisted of . . .

"How can I help you?" I asked.

"I am a member of a sky-diving team, and our team would like to sky dive into your brothel and spend some time with your ladies. It has always been a dream of ours since we discovered your website. Do you think something like that would be possible?"

"Sure, anything is possible here. You could sky dive into our courtyard, but we do have a pool in the center of the courtyard."

"That would be no problem. We're pretty good. I'm sure we will miss the pool."

We set it up. They would sky dive in the next weekend.

When I told the ladies about our sky divers, they were just like little kids, jumping around and giggling. The simplest things would excite them.

The weekend came. On schedule, we looked up to the sky and faintly saw six dots heading our way. Everyone was out in the courtyard, the ladies, the staff, and even some of our customers. The dots grew larger as they got closer and then we could make out the forms of the six sky divers. The ladies snapped photos of our guests as they descended. One by one they started to land in the courtyard. They were pretty good; so far no one had landed in the pool. Oops, I spoke too soon! Well, only one out of six landed in the pool. Not bad. The ladies ran over and helped them gather up their chutes.

"Thank you so much, madam. It was exhilarating. It was just like we imagined it would be. Now all we have to do is get a beer from your bar, spend some money on your ladies, and you'll make our dreams come true." I bought them all a drink in the bar and the ladies took it from there.

They had a great time. The customers and the staff got a free air show, the ladies partied, and I, well, I just chalked up another dream come true.

One day I received a call from a local radio station. They had a loyal listener who was terminally ill with cancer. The radio station had agreed to fulfill a wish for him. The deejay who called me said that Brad's wish was to visit a brothel and party with one of the ladies before he passes. Brad was given only a month to live. "We have collected five hundred dollars for Brad to spend," he said. Could we help fulfill Brad's wish?

"You bet. We'll send our limo to pick him up at your station and have our finest champagne chilled in the limo for him. Don't worry, we'll take really good care of Brad."

When Brad arrived at the brothel, he wasn't what I had expected to see. Brad was a young, handsome man. He couldn't have been older than thirty-five. He used a wheelchair, but you could tell that at one time he was extremely physically fit. His arms were still big, but most of his muscle mass had deteriorated. He was grateful, charming, and had a great sense of humor. The ladies all fell in love with him.

We had a lineup for Brad and he picked Winter, a beautiful brunette with long, straight hair that fell to her waist. Even though Brad had only five hundred dollars, he partied in a villa with Winter. We served them steak and lobster and sent out more of our finest champagne. After their party, which lasted quite a while, Brad, Winter, and the other ladies sat in the bar, drank, talked, and laughed for hours.

Winter came to the office and asked me if it would be all right to give Brad back his five hundred dollars. "Of course we can, if that is what you want," I said.

"Mom, I don't want to take his money. I would really like to give it back to him. I can't believe he is going to die; he's so young." Tears were streaming down Winter's face.

"I know, sweetheart, sometimes life seems so cruel, but just think of how happy you made Brad," I said. A big smile broke through her tears. She gathered up Brad's money and gave it back to him.

I walked out to the limo with Brad and he couldn't stop thanking me. "You don't know how much this meant to me. I've always wanted to visit a brothel and I always thought I had plenty of time to do it. I can't thank you enough. I will always remember you as the madam who made my dream come true."

The brothel offered many different things to many different people. It offered a safe alternative to couples who wanted to explore new options without risking the loss of friendships. It offered a legal alternative to customers who were looking for thrills and excitement. It offered a viable alternative to the disabled segment of our society. It offered the building of self-esteem and self-worth to those who felt inferior. It offered a learning experience for those who have never been with a woman before. It offered an opportunity to fulfill dreams and fantasies. It offered a fun working environment for the staff and a safe haven for the ladies. But most important, it offered safety and security to all who used it. When people think of brothels, they think of "sex for money," but what the customer is really paying for is the safety and security that accompanies the sex.

Looking back, it was plain to see why everyone enjoyed working at the brothel as much as they did. It made you feel good seeing people leave with big smiles on their faces. It made you feel good knowing that you played a small part in someone's happiness.

With everything that the brothel offered to its customers, there was one common denominator: It made dreams come true. Dreams of sexual fantasies, dreams of discovery, dreams of excitement, dreams of thrills, dreams of acceptance, dreams of self worth, dreams of happiness. We were the dream makers.

Hmmm. "Madam Dream Maker."

Chapter Nineteen

So Close, Yet So Far

Well, we did it. We transformed those three dirty little trailers into a multimillion-dollar resort. We set precedents in the industry. We did everything that everyone said couldn't be done. And once we did it, we expanded it, adding the hotel and spa. That, too, we were told, wouldn't fly.

The ladies were truly befitting of the name. They were, without a doubt, all ladies. They were beautiful and charming, well spoken, had great personalities, and were masters of the art of customer service.

The staff had transformed to a staff of resort quality. They anticipated the needs of customers. A customer didn't have to ask for anything and he didn't have to wait for anything. The staff was proactive, attentive, and caring.

It took years of hard work, training, counseling, dedication, and sometimes tears, but I made it through. Hell, I almost got divorced twice over that place. My husband, as understanding as he is, at times couldn't cope with the endless hours I put into that place. But just like the brothel, we made it, too.

It seemed to be all worthwhile. Business was good, and the facility was even better. The ladies were happy and the staff was content, but more importantly, the numbers were climbing. Our numbers at the brothel made it possible for the owners to spawn two more businesses in Las Vegas. The rate of growth over a few years' time was incredible. Most businesses would have been ecstatic to have our growth rate, not only in revenues, but in additional business properties.

Building that brothel was like raising a child. I watched it grow, I watched it develop, I watched it fall and was there to pick it up and dust it off. I watched it reach a potential that exceeded everyone's expectations. It was wonderful; it was my baby.

But internal politics began rearing their ugly head. I was always content at my brothel out in the middle of nowhere. But that wasn't the case in the corporate office and the other two businesses in Las Vegas. Everyone was jockeying for position. Everyone wanted to be a boss. Everyone wanted to be a big shot. It always amazed me how people would turn on one another for personal gain. I'd seen it thousands of times in the casino industry, and that's probably why I was so content at the brothel.

In all my years in the work force, I've never cared how much money someone else made or what title they had. They weren't putting any of their money in my account, so why should I care? As long as I could pay my bills, provide for my family, and take care of my dogs, I was happy. I had never been a "keep up with the Joneses" type.

A lot of my friends had big, beautiful showcase homes, and if that is what you like, then that is what you should have. I was never that type. I lived in a nice house, a small house but a nice house. I've always needed more space outside than I did inside. Those huge dogs of mine needed space! My St. Bernard weighed two hundred and twenty pounds! (I've always had a great fondness for any animal that weighed more than me!) I've always felt that the family could adjust, but the dogs, well, they had to have the room they needed. After all, humans have the ability to reason, right?

It was apparent that not too many in the company that I worked for possessed the ability to reason, at least not anymore. The company had gone through a transition of its own, and it wasn't for the better.

Success has a tendency to go to people's heads, and that seemed to be the case throughout the company. I was grateful to be in the middle of nowhere.

Battles were brewing. It was apparent that everyone in the company wanted to be a director of something or a vice president of something. Helloooooo, we're in the adult entertainment business; this isn't Microsoft. Corporate America had its place, but it wasn't in a brothel!

I kept to myself, running my brothel, trying to avoid all the back-stabbing and plotting that was taking place around me. It was crazy. Everyone was pointing fingers, placing blame. When did they have time to actually do the jobs they were hired for? I had more than enough to do just doing my job. Who had time for that crap? Evidently, everyone else.

The brothel staff noticed it, too. They frequently would ask me what was going on. We would all receive the e-mails that said, "So and so has left the company. We wish him the best of luck with all his future endeavors" or, "Please join us in congratulating so and so on his promotion to director of . . . or vice president of. . . ."

Are you kidding me? Vice president! Were we creating another nation? Vice president of what? Porn, sex, internal affairs? No, I've got it: Vice president of external affairs. Doesn't that sound impressive!

Things had finally fallen into place at the brothel and now this crap? I couldn't believe what was happening, and I was praying that we would be left out of it. This went on for months. So far, the brothel had managed to stay out of the line of fire. But how long would that last? Those people were on a mission. They wanted to rule the world!

Layers of titles and positions were created. We had vice presidents, who needed directors under them, who needed managers under them, who needed assistant managers under them, who needed supervisors under them. The list seemed endless.

Where was the staff? Everyone had a title, but where were the workers, the real people who got things done? Those people with their important titles didn't get anything done. They had much more important things to do with their time. They had to pass out their new business cards, with their fancy new titles on them. They had to take long, leisurely lunches. They had to interrupt a conversation you might be having to take a call on their BlackBerry. After all, it was an important call. That's what all important people do.

How had we survived without them? How did we muddle through life? How did we function day in and day out? How did we manage to build what we had built without all those titles?

Sooner or later, I knew this nonsense would spill over to the brothel. It was only a matter of time. It was a fear that would grow to consume me. Just as I watched the brothel grow, I was watching the birth of what could destroy it.

All these new vice presidents and directors and what-not were kids! Don't get me wrong. I love young people and I love to watch them grow and develop to their potential. But it's a process; it isn't something that happens overnight. You couldn't be a cook in a dumpy little bar one day and become a food and beverage director the next. But that's exactly what happened.

Sam befriended a cook in a seedy little beer joint. The next thing I knew, he had hired that cook and made him the food and beverage director at the brothel. That was the beginning of the long road to demise.

I'll never forget the day Sam called me to tell me the news. "I hired a food and beverage director for the brothel. He'll be starting on Monday."

"Food and beverage director?! We sell hamburgers and beer. What kind of director do we need for hamburgers and beer?"

There was no turning Sam around on this. He had made his decision; hell, he already had this guy processed and on the payroll. There was no discussion; this was simply a courtesy call from Sam so I wouldn't be wondering who the hell this guy was when he showed up on Monday.

Monday came around and so did the food and beverage director. I took one look at the guy and thought: You've got to be kidding! He didn't have a patch of skin on him that wasn't tattooed. I guess appearances didn't matter anymore for a resort! I kept looking at the guy as if I knew him from somewhere. But where? His name was Charles. That, too, sounded familiar. Where the hell did I know him from? One thing I did know was that I was positive we didn't run in the same social group.

Charles seemed friendly enough, but there was something about him that I never liked, aside from his tattoos. You know that feeling you get when something about someone bothers you but you can't put your finger on it? Well, that's the feeling I had, all the time, about Charles.

Sam and Charles were asshole buddies. Charles came to the brothel only once or twice a week. Some food and beverage director; he was a phantom! He got paid for forty hours a week even though we only saw him maybe six. Nice work if you can get it, I guess. I've always wanted a job like that: a part-time job with full-time pay, with benefits, of course. Later on, I would come to know exactly what those benefits included.

Charles, I was told, worked primarily out of the corporate office, although no one there really knew him to do any actual work. Of course not, he was a director.

Charles and Sam took long, leisurely lunches together. They played golf, went to bars — you know, all the things that important people do during their regularly scheduled work hours. My biggest fears were coming to fruition.

Sam just raved to Shawn about Charles. He was the greatest thing since sliced bread. Why wouldn't Sam think the world of Charles? Sam now had someone to pal around with. Shawn, who never spent a lot of time at the brothel, had no reason to question what Sam was saying.

The kitchen staff was not impressed with Charles either. They weren't happy anymore. They complained to me about the changes that were being made with their schedules, about the changes in purchasing lower grades of meats, and about how Charles spoke to them. "He is degrading. He told us we were stupid. We've been working here for quite some time and we've never had any complaints from any customers about the food, the quality, or the service, including the villas. We've prepared gourmet meals for the villas and there never has been one complaint." They were right. We never did receive any complaints about the food from anyone.

Sam didn't want to hear it. Charles was the golden child. Sam's response was, "If they don't like it, they can leave." Nice. I finally had built a good team, and one by one the kitchen staff began to quit. Charles hired new cooks and, oh yes, an executive chef. What else would you expect? And boy, talk about a motley crew. What a mess!

The ladies began to complain about the food. Sam didn't want to hear that either. This was the ladies' home; they were entitled to a decent meal. That didn't make a difference to Sam, or to Charles, for that matter. Neither one of them cared and they were quite blunt about it. So the ladies started buying their own food when they would go on their four hours out. I bought a freezer for them to store their food. I bought them a hotplate and pans to cook their food. Was I the only one who saw something wrong with this picture? Apparently so.

People fail to recognize the "snowball effect." Everything is relevant. First, you bring in this director, then the treatment of the kitchen staff sucks, then the kitchen staff quits, then you hire new kitchen staff and your executive chef, then the food sucks, then the ladies complain, then the ladies buy their own food and cook for themselves just to get a decent meal. Does anybody see a pattern here?

The rest of the staff was becoming jittery. They had witnessed the turnover of personnel in the kitchen. They didn't know what this new director was doing other than screwing everything up, and the ladies were complaining to them as well. Believe me, the ladies would complain to anyone with a set of ears! "What is happening here?" they would ask me.

"I'm not sure but corporate calls it progress."

Meanwhile, we were receiving e-mails with announcements of more promotions and more employees who had left the company. Everyone who had left seemed to be replaced by a director or a vice president. Unbelievable.

Each week I would contact the people I knew in the casino industry and get the occupancy rates of the hotels for that week. I would use that information to estimate what volume of business we could expect at the brothel. If their occupancy was high and they had promotions going on for their high-rollers, we could expect to be busier than normal. Of course, during events like the Super Bowl and the National Finals Rodeo, the brothel would always do well because every casino had its "whales" in town for those events.

One day I was talking to a friend of mine at one of the casinos and I brought up Charles' name. I told her that I couldn't figure out, for the life of me, where I knew him from. She enlightened me. "Remember when we used to work at that casino down on the far end of the Strip. Shit, it isn't there anymore. But anyway, he worked in the kitchen. Remember? There was a big 'to-do' and the cops came."

"That's right." I knew I recognized him. And then I knew what bothered me about him.

It was evident that Charles wasn't going anywhere, not in my lifetime anyway. Sam and Charles were inseparable. That's how Charles got his nickname: "Sam's Bitch." You didn't see one without the other.

The new kitchen staff liked Charles well enough. Why wouldn't they? Charles paid them more than the other employees were getting. How well do you think that went over with everyone else? I would try to get raises for other employees, the ones who had proven themselves, the ones who worked hard to preserve the reputation that the brothel had built. No luck. It seemed there wasn't enough money in the budget for them. I'm sure that with all the vice presidents, directors, and don't forget the executive chef, the U.S. Treasury would have a hard time covering that! Things weren't getting any better.

Time began to drag at the brothel. There was resentment among the staff about wages, the ladies were always complaining about the food, and then they started to complain about other things. One of the ladies who had been at the brothel for many years hadn't booked back in yet. That was odd. I called her to see if everything was all right.

"Denise, are you okay?"

"Oh, hi, Mom. Yes, I'm fine."

"I was worried because it's not like you to be gone from the brothel for so long."

"I know. I think it's time for a change."

"What's wrong?"

"Nothing, Mom, everything is fine, really."

Now, you know as well as I do that most times when you ask a woman what's wrong, she always says "nothing." But the way they say it tells you that "something" is wrong.

"Denise, you know you can tell me anything. You know I would do anything I could to help you. What is it, sweetheart?"

That is when I found out that Charles' benefits were more than your standard dental, health, and vision coverage. That bastard. He was putting pressure on the ladies, telling them that he was a friend of Sam's, and if they didn't have sex with him, he would have them fired. What a prick! I went ballistic when I found that out.

Now, how could I convince Sam that this was taking place? If he didn't want to hear about the old kitchen staff being unhappy, he certainly wouldn't want to hear about this. The timing had to be just right. Sam would have to be in the right frame of mind to hear something like this. Hell, as long as I'd known Sam, I don't think I'd ever seen him in the "right frame of mind." Can't at least one thing in my life ever be easy?

As time passed what I knew about Charles ate at me. I couldn't stand the sight of him. His mere presence would make me sick. During his weekly visit, he would flirt with all the ladies as Sam sat at the bar. Sam saw the same thing I did, but he didn't seem to care.

This brothel had set the standard. Were we going to revert back to the old ways of the industry? Mauling and pawing the ladies and forcing them to do things they didn't want to do just to save their jobs? Over my dead body! We had all worked too hard to overcome the raunchy side of the business. What the hell could they be thinking? It was the adage of "the little head telling the big head what to do." Men shouldn't have anything to do with this business; they have no self-control.

When we started, Sam was in my corner. He felt the same way I did. He was adamant that no one, other than a customer, was to touch any of the ladies. I guess it was easier then, when the ladies resembled anything but a lady. But now, these ladies were classy and gorgeous. The only way Charles could possibly get a lady of that caliber was to threaten her, hold something over her head, or use his position (which was a joke to begin with) to force her to succumb to him. What an asshole!

I knew from previous experience that saying anything about Charles to Sam was a waste of time. So, I turned to Shawn instead. I told Shawn what was going on. He wasn't too happy about what he was hearing.

"I'll speak to Sam and it will be taken care of." Good enough for me.

The next weekly visit came and I didn't notice any change in Charles' behavior. I called Shawn. "Did you speak with Sam?"

"About what?" Are you kidding me? "About Charles. About him screwing all of your ladies. Does any of this ring a bell?"

"Oh, yeah. I mean, no; I forgot."

"It's really important. I need you to speak with Sam. This has got to stop now!"

"Okay, I will."

Shawn must have finally said something to Sam, because Sam's attitude changed dramatically. He was standoffish and wouldn't speak to me unless he absolutely had to. I'd known Sam for at least ten years. This was totally out of character for him. What the hell could be the attraction between him and Charles? It had to be something else. Oh, well, all I cared about were my ladies. Charles cooled his jets and that was the goal I wanted to accomplish.

Business at the brothel was good. I was booking in a lot of ladies from the Northern Nevada brothels. Our brothel had the reputation of being second to none and ladies who had worked up north started to venture down our way. They would walk into the brothel and their jaws would drop. "I had no idea it was this nice. I looked at your website, but really, the site doesn't do justice to this place. It is beautiful." I would beam as if my child had just graduated from Harvard.

The brothels in Northern Nevada operated quite different from the brothels in Southern Nevada. Most of the Northern brothels had escort licenses as well, so their ladies could leave the brothel with a customer for a "date." They would go to dinner, or gamble at a nearby casino, or take in a movie. It was perfectly legal up north. But the ordinances that governed the Southern Nevada brothels didn't permit that.

A lot of the customers followed their favorite ladies and visited them at my brothel. They would be disappointed to learn that they couldn't take the lady out for a "date." It was always my goal to satisfy every customer, but the Northern Nevada customers were a challenge. I couldn't change the laws and I certainly wouldn't consider violating them. There must be something I could do. I thought about it for a while, weeks actually, and then it came to me. If they want to take their lady out for a fine dinner, they should be able to, right? Absolutely! Then they shall.

I started drawing up some plans, projecting costs and crunching numbers. I could do this and it would cost only about fifteen hundred dollars. Of course, I was factoring in my husband's help and I didn't pay him nearly enough for the work — and the quality of work — that he did for the brothel. But business was business and I needed to keep the costs down.

I called Sam even though we weren't on the best of terms; it was the right thing to do. After all, I still worked for the guy. "Sam, I have an idea to generate more revenue. We have an empty office right next to one of the ladies' rooms and I want to turn it into a specialty party room. I want to make it into a fine dining room."

"Why would you want to do that? We have the villas if someone wants food during their party."

"It's not about the food; it's about taking the lady out for dinner. We are competing with the brothels up north and our customers want to be able to take their lady out, too. Look, I can build and furnish this room, elegantly, for about fifteen hundred dollars. What do you say?"

"Well, do it if you want to, but I don't think it's going to fly."

Haven't I heard that somewhere before?

Later that night, Shawn called just to chat. He would do that a lot. Everyone else he dealt with in the business told Shawn what he wanted to hear. I told him the way it was. I think he respected that. He would call and sometimes we would talk for hours, just shooting the shit. I'd always make him laugh. I believe that each day you do not laugh, you've wasted a day. Even with all the garbage that was going on within the company, I never wasted a day.

I was so excited about the fine dining room and began rattling off all my plans. Shawn laughed.

"What's so funny?"

"I knew it wasn't Sam's idea," he said. "I haven't known Sam to come up with any ideas before, and it struck me kind of odd that he would now, but I figured, well, maybe he's taking a proactive approach. I should have known better."

That bastard tried to steal credit for my idea! "He pitched the fine dining room to you as his own?"

"Yeah, isn't that funny?"

"Hysterical. Anyhow, so what do you think of the idea; my idea?"

"Do you think it will work?" Shawn asked.

"It will when people find out what we're going to serve for dessert!"

"Sam didn't mention that part."

"That's because I didn't tell Sam that part. Once I got his okay, I was off and running."

"So, what's for dessert?"

"Okay, picture this. You're having a wonderful gourmet dinner with a beautiful lady. The room is absolutely gorgeous; soft lighting from a crystal chandelier, walls in a dark, rich chocolate color on the lower third and a rich gold-tone suede finish on the top two-thirds, beautiful artwork magnificently framed, marble server with two buffet lamps with a soft, low glow, Waterford vase with fresh flowers. Sound good?"

"Sounds great!"

"You're looking across the table, which is draped in a rich hunter-green fabric that meets the floor, and is set with fine white china with a thin, gold trim, gold ware, crystal champagne glasses and water goblets, and you are totally intoxicated by your lady's beauty. Dinner is served and your casual conversation and laughter drowns out the soft piano music playing in the background. After dinner and a bottle of champagne, it's time to serve dessert. Your beautiful lady seductively slips down from her chair and disappears under the table. You slide back in your chair and, to your surprise, you're enjoying a sensual dessert, prepared especially for you!"

"Oh yeah, that will work. What a great idea!"

"You can't get a dessert like that in any other restaurant, not without being arrested!" I said.

I got to work on the fine dining room. Fernando helped me clear out the office. I bought the paint, crown molding and chair rail so my husband and Fernando could get started. Fernando painted, my husband did all the woodwork, and I shopped. What a team! I bought new carpet, fabric for the drapes and the table, furniture, accessories, and, don't forget, the chandelier. It was beautiful with teardrop crystals and crystal-draped beading. Oh, this was going to look fabulous.

Every night after working at his shop, my husband came to the brothel and worked on the dining room. You gotta love this guy! The painting was done, the wood trim was done, and the carpeting was in. The room took shape.

All the staff and ladies were curious to know what was going on. When the room was completed, I would tell them all about it. Until then, they'd just have to speculate. Rumors were flying around the house: The madam is moving her office; no, she is building a "negotiation room"; no, it's going to be a reception area . . . and so on.

The room was completed about a month later. It was time for the unveiling. I met with the staff first. All of the staff would be involved with the success of this room. The bar would prepare the drinks, security would deliver them, the shift managers would take the orders and book the party, the kitchen would prepare the food, and housekeeping would clean the room and reset the table. The staff was enthusiastic. They were team players and couldn't wait to book a party in the dining room.

At first, the ladies were hesitant. They couldn't understand the concept.

"Why wouldn't we just book a villa?"

I explained: "A lot of our Northern customers are accustomed to taking ladies out of the house on a date. Now, they can take you ladies out for dinner within the guidelines that we are governed by. Also, remember, ladies, not all customers can afford a villa party. The dining room will give them another option and give you another opportunity to up-sell. The minimum on the dining room will be one thousand dollars. You would be giving a blow job for a thousand-dollar minimum. It also gives you an option when you have a customer who is adamant about spending time with you."

Many other brothels sold their services by time. Their parties would be negotiated by time; the ladies would negotiate by the half hour or hour. But this brothel was different. We didn't sell time, we sold activity.

Once the ladies heard that they would get a thousand dollars, minimum, just for a blow job, they were excited, too. It all goes back to putting things in a perspective people can relate to. The ladies related to money extremely well!

Alice was the first lady to book the dining room. She booked it for four thousand dollars. At the beginning, the dining room parties were a little rocky, from the staff's standpoint. But just like with the villas, it didn't take too long before booking the dining room was an ordinary occurrence.

We booked seventy-two thousand dollars in revenue the first month alone. Alice's first dining room party more than paid for the cost of the room. I spent seventeen hundred dollars, total, to build that room. What a great idea Sam had. The guy has to be a genius.

The following month, the dining room booked eighty-four thousand dollars. Why didn't I think of this years ago? It was unbelievable. Who knew?

As time passed, Sam became a little friendlier toward me, but it still wasn't the same. I just went on doing my job, maintaining control of the house and making money. Sam's friendlier attitude didn't last too long, though. He sent me an e-mail stating that he did not want the brothel to host luncheons or tours anymore. His e-mail stated that he believed the brothel was losing customers because of the tours. What an idiot!

The tours took place during the late morning and early afternoon hours, not exactly the time of day when the brothel business was at its peak. Although the brothel business was a spontaneous business and there really was no true trend as to when the peak hours were, it definitely wasn't during the lunch hour. The evening hours and swing shifts were apt to be busier than most others. However, occasionally we'd have a day shift or graveyard shift that would be stronger than a swing shift. Sometimes we would have a Tuesday that was stronger than a Saturday.

Regardless, we weren't losing customers because of the tours. Our customer count had declined a bit, but that was attributed to the illegal prostitution running wild in Las Vegas, to excessive gasoline prices, and to the corporate office focusing on its two other businesses in Las Vegas. The brothel had become a redheaded stepchild. We made the money that spawned two new businesses, and now these vice presidents and directors were instructing their people to focus on those businesses. I couldn't convince anyone that the brothel website needed constant maintenance and updating. We got eighty percent of our customers from our website. How hard was this to figure out?

"The other businesses aren't making money. We need to focus on them," was the standard answer from Sam and Shawn. So, focus on them and stop sending me stupid e-mails!

The tours stopped. I tracked the customer count for one year after we stopped the tours. Our customer count didn't go up. I knew the tours had nothing to do with the customer count! The only effect that discontinuing the tours had on the brothel was that our retail revenue declined and so did bar revenue. Those tours spent thousands of dollars in our gift shop and they purchased a lot of drinks. Yup, Sam was a genius.

Many people were disappointed that we didn't offer tours anymore. Practically every day I received a phone call from one group or another that wanted to book a luncheon and tour. After a while, the word got out and the phone calls stopped. Had they forgotten about all the perceptions that we had changed over the years? Had they forgotten that it was the Red Hats, who were our biggest tour groups and apparently our biggest fans, who saved our asses during that whole political fiasco? It never ceased to amaze me how quickly people forget what and who contributed to their success. I guess, after a while, after you become successful, you truly believe that you did it all by yourself. That's arrogant and stupid.

The ladies also were disappointed that the tours had stopped. It was a refreshing change for them. It broke up the monotony of their day. Since they lived at the brothel for two or three weeks at a time, some even longer, the tours provided them with a change of scenery.

The ladies' day consisted primarily of sitting in the bar waiting for a prospective customer to come in; that is, when they didn't have any appointments scheduled. The ladies developed friendships among themselves, so they would sit in the bar with one or two other ladies and shoot the shit until a likely candidate ambled in. That routine got real old real fast. How many hours could you sit and talk to the same people, about the same things, day after day? The tours gave them an opportunity to speak with new people about new things. Yes, it was a refreshing change of scenery for the ladies.

The bartenders missed the tours, too. They would make great tips from those tours. Believe me, they worked for every penny of it. Some of the tour groups were quite large. As I recall, the largest group we had was one hundred and ten people. It was hectic, to say the least, but it was worth it. I broke the group down into four smaller groups for the tours to make sure everyone saw and heard everything and to make sure that I answered everyone's questions. They spent over two thousand dollars that day in the gift shop. Not too bad!

When they learned that we weren't offering tours anymore, the Red Hats came in and bought the remaining Red Hat T-shirts and mugs that we had in stock. They've become collector's items now.

The brothel was heading in a new direction. I didn't particularly think it was a better direction, but it was definitely a new direction. The other businesses and the corporate office were still going through their growing pains. I would stop by the corporate office on occasion, and I wouldn't know half the people there anymore. Where did all these people come from? And what do they do? It was certainly quite different from when we started with the original five people who constituted the corporate office. There had to be thirty of them packed in there now.

The staff at the brothel was becoming more and more nervous. They weren't opposed to change, either. We'd all been through nothing but change since the brothel's inception. But this new direction we were headed in didn't seem to be benefiting the brothel. It only seemed to be benefiting all the vice presidents and directors.

It was becoming a never-ending game of Pass the Buck. Any time the brothel needed something, anything, whether it was new information to be posted on the website or more postage for the postage meter, it didn't matter what it was, I would have to talk to at least five different people, only to get the same response from each of them: "Oh, I don't do that. You'll have to talk to so-and-so." Who the hell was so-and-so? I must have missed that e-mail!

This place was turning into a nightmare. Every time you spoke with someone, it was always the same: "That's not my job." What happened to internal customer service? What happened to taking ownership of a problem? It took an act of Congress to get anything accomplished anymore. And try to schedule a meeting with someone to try to get something resolved. They were all too busy. "I couldn't possibly meet with you this week. I'm just buried."

I'd like to bury them all! I couldn't believe what was happening.

Maybe it was just me. Maybe I was just too set in my ways. Maybe I was from the old school and this was how things are done now. Maybe this was the way of the future. Things have changed a lot in the business world since I started working in it.

I never used to get e-mails. If I wanted to speak with someone, I just picked up the phone and called him. Now, if I pick up the phone, I don't talk to anyone, I get a recording! Press one for English, press two for customer service, press three if you're a vendor, and on and on. I'm taking orders from an electronic device.

And the cell phone, well, it wasn't just a phone anymore. I got my e-mails on it. It was an electronic leash. The phone didn't know the difference between the middle of the day and the middle of the night and neither did the idiot on the other end who was sending me an e-mail. That thing would chirp all night long!

Was it possible? Could it be I was getting old? I don't mean old in age, I mean old in my thoughts? Was I turning into my mother? Was I going to start telling my children, "I remember walking to school two miles each way, in the snow, uphill both ways"?

Oh, hell no. That wasn't going to happen to me! I have to adopt a younger thought process. I have to embrace this change. Who knows, maybe it would be better. Maybe this was the way business was supposed to work nowadays. I am open-minded. Perhaps it wouldn't be such a bad thing. I wasn't sure what the company had in mind as far as this new direction they were headed in, but what the hell, we'll give it a shot. We could always change back, right?

My mind was racing with all sort of thoughts, and then it dawned on me: I was trying to convince myself that these changes would be an improvement. My mind was desperately trying to override what I knew in my heart.

Chapter Twenty

Hanging Up my Hat

The internal battle between my heart and my head raged for months. My mind desperately tried to convince my heart that a new direction may not be such a terrible thing. It could be a refreshing change; a new direction may bring forth exciting opportunities, new avenues to explore. Give it a shot. Several years back, I didn't know a thing about brothels; look at it as a learning experience. What's the worst that could happen? It doesn't work and we make more changes. Shawn was a very smart businessman. Surely he wouldn't allow anything to have an adverse affect on his income. That just wouldn't be smart business. If this new direction adversely affected his money, he would make the necessary adjustments to combat that, right? I could live with that.

New Year's was just around the corner and I was looking forward to it. Maybe "sanity" would be Sam's New Year's resolution and all this craziness would come to a screeching halt.

Shawn called to wish me a happy new year. "This year is going to be our best year ever," he said.

"I hope so," I responded. "I really hope so."

New Year's was typically a quiet night at the brothel. No one could compete with Las Vegas on New Year's Eve, not even prostitution.

Our bar regulars would come in and visit with the ladies. We had tiaras and hats and noisemakers to bring in the new year and the ladies always got a kick out of taking off the customers' cowboy hats and replacing them with those ridiculous foil-like top hats. At midnight I would break out bottles of champagne and everyone would make a toast. One of our regular customers stood up on the bar to make a toast: "To my favorite madam, who makes every day feel like a holiday."

"Here, here!" shouted the crowd.

"I'll drink to that," I said, and we did.

New Year's has always been one of my favorite holidays. It is a holiday of new beginnings, anticipation and renewed hopes. That's why so many people make resolutions. It's a conscious decision to make the new year better than the year before. After all, isn't that what we all want, everything to be better?

So, my resolution was to make decisions that would make things better for my ladies and better for me. My outlook on things was upbeat and positive. I made my resolution; I made a promise to myself. Things would be better, one way or another.

It seems during the holiday season that people make an extra effort to be a little friendlier, a little more cordial, a little more caring, a little more compassionate, a better person. I've always thought that it should be that way every day, not just during the holidays. That's what I believe, that's how I live. And some people notice; some people really do take notice. Perhaps their noticing prompted the customer's New Year's toast, "To my favorite madam, who makes every day feel like a holiday."

The holiday season departed as quickly as it came and that extra effort left even more quickly. Things went back to the way they had been without skipping a beat. Charles was out of control, and with others in the company on his bandwagon, it was downright ugly. The benefits packages that apparently some of the executives received — well, you wouldn't find them in any employee handbook. New hot shots kept infiltrating the company. Everyone was desperately trying to make a name for himself. But there was so much they needed to learn first. Hey, what a concept: Why not learn the job first and then try to make improvements? I suppose my way of thinking was antiquated, as it was evident that his new corporate thought process was to first "act" and then "think."

So, along with the new year and the new direction came new personnel and new ideas. Policies were being changed and everyone, including this madam, would learn of them through e-mails. We started receiving e-mails from people we had never heard of before. Who were these people?

The medication policy was changed and now the ladies had total control over their meds. The new policy stated that the ladies could take their medication as often as they wanted and take as many as they wanted. We could no longer dispense meds to them. It didn't take long before one lady overdosed. I received a phone call in the middle of the night from a hysterical shift manager.

"Call 911, I'm on my way!" I said.

The brothels were hesitant to call the police, paramedics, or any other emergency services. Of course we did in the event of an emergency, such as the overdose, but as a general rule the brothels would call 911 only as a last resort. We put procedures in place to avoid these types of situations, but these new policy changes made that impossible.

It all had to do with politics. Everyone in this rural town had a scanner and they would listen to all the emergency calls. During an election year, politicians who weren't in favor of legalized prostitution would use that information against the brothels. "The brothels had the police out there nine times. They had the fire department out there twice and the paramedics out there half a dozen times. They are a nuisance. They have nothing but trouble out there. Each time an emergency unit is dispatched to the brothels is just one more call that may have to wait for us decent citizens."

"Decent," can you believe it? That's all it took and once again the brothels were under fire. Comments of that nature became ammunition to be used against legal prostitution. The brothel business was such a volatile business. One unjust comment was all it would take to put the entire community into a feeding frenzy.

Procedures were put in place for these specific reasons. Not only to protect the ladies, but to protect the industry as a whole. This new company direction was taking its toll on everyone.

The battle within me raged on. I began to reassess whether this hell I was going through would be worth the fight. I had developed a reputation in the industry of being the madam of the new millennium, the madam who introduced respectability and compassion to the industry, the madam who changed perceptions. Now we were being labeled indecent?

Phone calls started coming in from other brothel madams. "What the hell is going on down there? We're being persecuted by the politicians, by the press, by everyone; what is happening?" Those were good questions, but this madam didn't have the answers; not this time.

No one seemed to be even the slightest bit disturbed by the events taking place at the brothel. No one other than myself and the other brothel madams. The overdose was just the beginning.

Now that Charles' "benefits" had kicked back in, and other company executives were following in his footsteps, it didn't take long before the brothel got the reputation of the old Hollywood days when the "casting couch" determined whether one would be considered for the part. The ladies were being "auditioned" by multiple levels of executives, from the higher-ups all the way down to the food and beverage director.

Perhaps the politicians knew of this, and if so, then they were right. These weren't decent people. "Decent" is defined as "polite, honest, civilized, well-brought-up, well-mannered, respectable." These people didn't possess any of those qualities.

There was no doubt about it: This "new direction" was reverting the industry back to what it was. This new direction was taking us back to where we started. What the hell were they thinking?

For the next few months, the turmoil within me grew. I watched as the baby I had nurtured was being tormented, abused . . . destroyed. I had numerous conversations with Shawn, as he was the only one, I thought, who could stop this madness. "I don't think I can do this anymore. Everyone has a saturation point and I think I have reached mine," I told him.

"You can't leave me," Shawn said. "You're my wingman. Things will get better. Just hang in there and they will get better, trust me."

I've always trusted Shawn. He never gave me a reason not to.

Time dragged on and the morale of the staff and ladies dragged right along with it. The brothel, once considered an icon in the industry, was developing a new reputation and was quickly becoming the "black eye" of the industry.

The ladies weren't comfortable anymore. I found myself spending most of my days giving the ladies pep talks. The pep talk I would give to myself was proving to be disastrous and I could only hope that the ones I gave to the ladies would have better results. Do you know how hard it was to convince someone that everything would be fine when you knew in your heart that it wouldn't? I was trying to convince the ladies of something that I no longer believed myself. I was lying to them. Had this brothel been reduced to operating based on a pack of lies? Dewey would have been so disappointed.

The locals felt it the most. You could cut the tension with a knife. The corporate gurus made it clear that locals were no longer welcome at the brothel. Our neighborhood bar no longer welcomed the neighborhood. A cease and desist was put on all promotions geared toward the local clientele. No more "Monday Night Football," no more Super Bowl parties, no more anything.

"Sam, what is going on? We can't discontinue our promos for the locals. That's suicide!"

Sam wasn't interested. "The locals don't spend any money in the brothel. We have no reason to continue to cater to them. They're not worth it."

"Not worth it? They're the ones who vote. They're the ones who keep us in business. They're the ones who determine if we exist or if we don't exist!"

"Our vice president of finance says the numbers don't gel," Sam said. "We're spending money on something that gives us a zero return. We're not doing it anymore."

Vice president of finance . . . I have outfits older than this guy! What the hell does he know? It was more than obvious. Stupid was running rampant within the company. How do you overcome stupidity? How do you combat that? There is no cure for stupid.

"What is happening here?" local after local asked. That became the million-dollar question. I knew how fragile the brothel and its reputation were. As any good mother would, I did whatever it took to protect my baby, to present an image of decency, to be a good neighbor in my community. I knew there would always be attacks from those who did not approve, did not understand, or would not take the time to learn what brothels really offered, but I never dreamed that we would be attacked from within. I never imagined that we would face "friendly fire."

Who would have thought that anything like this would be going on behind the scenes at a brothel? We sold sex; it wasn't quantum physics. How difficult could it be? You would expect to see this type of politics in a casino, in a large corporation, but here? This wasn't the place for internal politics. We had plenty of battles to fight with the crusaders; we didn't need to fight among ourselves. This whole thing was beyond my scope of comprehension.

Time progressed, the madness progressed, and the brothel regressed. Things weren't getting better. I began questioning myself: How long are you going to stay and watch the property you have given birth to be destroyed?

It's kind of ironic. Over the years I had changed thousands of perceptions about the brothel, yet I couldn't change the perceptions among the people who were closest to it. The brothel had become their personal playground. Drugs were running rampant; they were even being supplied by some of the directors. What happened to the importance of "protecting the license"? Brothel licenses are privileged licenses. It was imperative to protect that license. That license was the foundation of our existence. Any findings of illegal drugs would surely result in the revocation of that license. Why was I the only one who was concerned about this?

I thought back to my conversation with Shawn. "You can't leave me, you're my wingman," he said. Wingman, my ass. I'm a kamikaze pilot.

It was at that moment I realized I had made my decision. I was not going to be part of this suicide mission. At that moment a sudden rush of relief came over me. The turmoil inside of me, the raging battle between head and heart, had vanished.

Yes, that's it. I had made my decision. I'm going to be like John Elway: I am going to leave while I am still at the top of my game.

The feeling of helplessness was gone. What was this? I felt good! My heart prevailed. It was the right decision; it was the right time. I did what I set out to do, I accomplished my goal. I had offered the best brothel, the best ladies, the best staff, the best customer service, the best environment, the best treatment the ladies had ever experienced, the best reputation, the best dreams! I did it! I won the Super Bowl, just like John Elway. And just like Elway, I'm going out on top. I'm hanging up my hat.

I called Shawn and told him of my decision. "You can't leave me," he said once more.

"I'm not leaving you, I'm just leaving," I said. The critical part of trying to be the best at what you do is knowing when to throw in the towel. Knowing when to make adjustments. Knowing the right thing and doing the right thing should always be one and the same; that's what this madam believes. That's what this madam had practiced and preached, until that little bump in the road with the battle between my heart and my head. What I do, I do with a passion. Passion comes from the heart, but it is because you believe. Beliefs come from the head. Your heart and head should always be in sync. And if they aren't, as they weren't for me for far too long, then it is time to make adjustments. That's smart business.

My head was clear. The confusion was gone. I had regained my direction. I had regained my focus and was heading forward at full throttle.

Still, there was a part of me that felt sorry for those new executives, those new vice presidents and directors. They lacked what this madam's generation was raised on: loyalty and integrity. They just didn't understand that you pass the same people going up the corporate ladder that you do on the way down.

This country was built on a handshake, when someone's word meant something. It's not just about money. It's about looking in the mirror every day and liking what you see. It's about knowing that the person looking back at you in that mirror is honest, respectable, dedicated, and a person of her word. This new generation seems to be all about fancy cars, fancy homes, and bling. But the person with the most toys doesn't win! It's how you play the game that counts, and I'm playing it with my heart.

I felt better than I had in months. I got some empty boxes and started packing up my office. As I was taking the pictures off my walls, I started experiencing a shift in my emotions. One by one, as I took the photos the ladies had signed to me off the wall and put them in the box, a feeling of sadness seeped in. Those ladies, they worm their way into your heart. They're beautiful and bright, they're sweet and sincere. They're adults who have managed to hang on to bits and pieces of youth. They're amazing.

I tried as hard as I could to leave unnoticed. The last thing I wanted was to cause any more drama in the house. There was certainly an abundance of that going around and I didn't want to add to it.

I carried one box out and when I came back in, the shift manager was crying so hard that she couldn't even answer the phone. It didn't take long before most everyone knew that I was leaving. The saying in Vegas is "What happens in Vegas, stays in Vegas" but the saying at the brothel was "What happens at the brothel goes around in five minutes." I don't even think it took that long. In a matter of seconds there were ladies in my office pleading for me to reconsider.

It broke my heart to listen to their pleas through their tearful sobbing. You know the kind of sobbing where you can't even catch your breath? These grown women could transform themselves into the likes of helpless children in the blink of an eye.

I tried to reassure them that everything would be fine.

"Mom, you can't leave us."

"What will we do without you?"

"We need you."

"Who will take care of us?"

"No one cares about us as much as you do."

I fought like hell to hold back my tears. The last thing they needed was for me to cave in. I was always strong for them. I was their rock and I'll be damned if I won't be rock solid until the end. I will see this thing through.

Walking out with the last box was the hardest. I had ladies grabbing on to me and holding on for dear life, crying and pleading and making a last-ditch effort to persuade me to stay. The ladies were like children caught in the crosshairs of a divorce. I put the box down, hugged them, gave them each a kiss and once again reassured them that everything would be fine. I thought, if I don't get out of this building in the next second or so, there will be no way I can maintain my composure.

As I drove out of the parking lot, I gazed in my rearview mirror. There they were, hugging, crying and trying to console one another. I could see tears glisten on their cheeks as they were caught in the sunlight. Those beautiful ladies. I was so grateful to have had the opportunity to know them.

As they vanished from sight, it was time for me to let go. The flow of tears was nonstop. I thought I was going to dehydrate through my eyes!

I reached over and shut off my cell phone. I knew soon there would be a series of phone calls and I wasn't up to reliving what had just taken place. Twenty-four hours of peace and quiet is what I needed. I was entitled to it.

Despite the mixed emotions, I knew I had made the right decision. I knew that as long as I stayed at the brothel, so would the ladies. They would endure the "auditions" because somehow, in their minds, they would justify it and know that I would be there to take care of them. There were twenty-four legal brothels throughout Nevada. Many of them had upgraded to the standards we had set. They would be better off in the long run. It was a decision that had to be made; for me and for them. Tough love: It's the hardest love to give, and, at the time, seems even harder to receive.

It didn't take long before most of the ladies had ventured off to other brothels. Just like everyone had her own reason for going to the brothel, everyone had her own reason for leaving the brothel. My reason? I never want to lose the passion. I always want to believe.

After all was said and done, I recognized that this was the opportunity of a lifetime. The world of legal prostitution — it wasn't just a job. Jobs are where you clock in, do your work, clock out, and live your life. The world of legal prostitution was nothing like that. It intertwined with your life. It was a process of slow osmosis, so slow that you do not realize it has crept its way into your life. There was no leaving the workplace, no forgetting about what took place during the course of the day, no picking up where you left off in your life. It *was* your life. It was phone calls in the middle of the night, every night. It was spending hours trying to console a grown woman who has lost custody of her children. It was sitting at her bedside, praying she pulls through. It was applying make-up to cover bruises. It was mending broken hearts. It was celebrating victories. It was comforting them through their defeats. It was picking them up. It was dusting them off. It was incredible.

The world of legal prostitution is a world of its own. Just think about how many women in this country can say they've been a madam? I am one of the few.

To this day, I still hear from my ladies. Those wonderful, drama-filled, chaotic ladies, my daughters throughout the world. They ran you through every emotion, from cheers to tears. I still help them through their trials and tribulations. I still comfort them when they are scared. I still advise them, counsel them, console them, and care for them. They call; we talk; we laugh. I will always be Mom to them and they will be forever in my heart.

The drive home seemed to take forever, even though I lived only ten minutes from the brothel. I was so consumed in thought that I didn't remember passing the pastures that I passed every day. I didn't remember seeing the horses and cows that I looked for in those pastures.

I dried my eyes and walked into my house. I kissed my dogs and it was as if they knew something was different. Usually they would jump over one another in an effort to be the first to greet their mommy, but today I greeted them. I put my purse down and sat down at the dining room table. My husband was there to lend his shoulder.

"Are you all right?" he asked.

"You know, I think I am." I lit a cigarette. "Oh wait, I have to do just one more thing." I got up, walked over to the entryway, and hung up my hat.

ACKNOWLEDGMENTS

Thank you to my husband, Kevin, who afforded me the endless hours of uninterrupted solitude I needed to accomplish this goal and for his unwavering support. He was a bachelor for many months during this project and discovered that he enjoyed married life so much more.

My three children, Jennifer, Michael, and Kevin, taught me to expect the unexpected, something that only teenagers can grant you a Ph.D. in. They have all grown up to be quite amazing adults, which only goes to show, once again, to expect the unexpected.

The working girls, industry-wide, gave me so many wonderful memories, which far outweighed the tears. They are remarkable and I am grateful to know them the way I do.

Also, thanks to Judi Moreo, who has inspired me to write and to share, encouraging me every step of the way; Fiona Carmichael, who helped me to realize that our dreams can be within our reach; Geoff Schumacher, who helped guide me through this project; and Carolyn Hayes Uber, who believed in me and helped my dream become a reality.

Thank you to my friends, in the West and the East, for their unconditional help and support.

ABOUT THE AUTHOR

Laraine Russo Harper served for six years as the madam of a well-known brothel in Pahrump, Nevada, sixty miles west of Las Vegas.

She spearheaded a dramatic transformation of the brothel from a dingy collection of trailers into a luxury resort. Harper no longer works in the industry but she still lives in Pahrump with her husband and seven dogs. This is her first book.